D0400620

SYLVIA PORTER'S YOUR FINANCIAL SECURITY

Other Avon Books by
Sylvia Porter

Sylvia Porter's A Home of Your Own
Sylvia Porter's Love and Money
Sylvia Porter's New Money Book for the 80's
Sylvia Porter's Your Own Money

Coming Soon

Sylvia Porter's Guide to Your Health Care

SYLVIA PORTER'S YOUR FINANCIAL SECURITY

Sylvia Porter

With the Contributors to <u>Sylvia Porter's Personal Finance Magazine</u>

AVON BOOKS  NEW YORK

This book is intended to provide general information. The publisher, authors, and copyright owner are not engaged in rendering personal finance, investment, tax, accounting, legal, or other professional advice and services and cannot assume responsibility for individual decisions made by readers.

Should assistance for these types of advice and services be required, professionals should be consulted.

References to tax provisions in this book are based on current tax laws and regulations. Revisions in tax law, if adopted, might affect the tax consequences.

AVON BOOKS
A division of
The Hearst Corporation
105 Madison Avenue
New York, New York 10016

Copyright © 1984, 1985, 1986, 1987 by Sylvia Porter's Personal Finance® Magazine Company
Book design by Beth McNally/McNally Graphic Design
Published by arrangement with the author
Library of Congress Catalog Card Number: 87-34988
ISBN: 0-380-89754-7

Published in hardcover by William Morrow and Company, Inc.; for information address Permissions Department, William Morrow and Company, Inc., 105 Madison Avenue, New York, New York 10016.

First Avon Books Trade Printing: September 1989

AVON TRADEMARK REG. U.S. PAT. OFF. AND IN OTHER COUNTRIES, MARCA REGISTRADA, HECHO EN U.S.A.

Printed in the U.S.A.

OPM 10 9 8 7 6 5 4 3 2 1

Acknowledgments

WE wish to express our appreciation and gratitude to the following authors who allowed us to include or to quote from the articles listed below. Most of the articles originally appeared in *Sylvia Porter's Personal Finance*® *Magazine:*

Marcia Ringer Barman for "Getting Coverage Despite Illness." Pamela J. Bayless for "Sheltering Sideline Income for Your Retirement." Eleanor Berman for "How Good Is Your Homeowner's Policy?" Warren Boroson for "How to Handle Any Financial Emergency." Patricia Schiff Estess for her contribution to "Financial Planning: A Lifetime Affair." Allen Evans for America's Money-Back Guarantee." Fred Gebhart for "Insurance You Don't Need" and "Liability Insurance: How Much Is Enough?" Ellen Goldschmidt for "Sensational Sidelines." Janis Graham for "The Facts of Life (Insurance)," "Protect Your Estate: 4 Ways to Cut Heirs' Tax Burden" and her contribution to "Financial Planning: A Lifetime Affair." Ellen Hermanson for "Securing the Future of a Disabled Child," "Safeguarding Your Money . . . in Annuities," and her contribution to "Financial Planning: A Lifetime Affair." Mike Hernacki for "Checking Out a Prospective Employer." Marilynn Larkin for her contribution to "How You Can Benefit from Today's Health Care Revolution." Elizabeth S. Lewin for "Putting Your Money to Work." Elana Lore for "The Golden Rules." Cindy McCartney for "Putting Your Home on the Line (of Credit)" and "Turn Your Home into a Cash Machine." Donald Nichols for "Managing Your Savings." Katharine Ramsden for "Safeguarding Your Money . . . in Municipal Bonds and Brokerage Houses." Arthur H. Rogoff as principal author of "Financial Planning: A Lifetime Affair." Lois Rosenthal for "Strategies for Career Changes." Alice Priest Shafran for "Helping Elderly Parents." Dana Shilling for

"Transferring Assets from One Generation to Another." Leonard Sloane for "It's Time for Your Annual Portfolio Checkup." Catherine Stribling for "Safeguarding Your Money . . . in Banks." Diane J. Wyle for "What Makes a Millionaire."

We'd like to extend a special thank-you to Ellen Goldschmidt, outside editor on this project; Arthur H. Rogoff, executive editor for SPPFM subsidiary products, who supplied vital assistance; and Meritta S. White, our tireless research fact-checker. Thanks, too, to Carole Sinclair, publisher and editorial director of SPPFM; Patricia Schiff Estess, editor of SPPFM; and Jeanette McClain, SPPFM assistant editor.

Contents

Introduction ◆◆◆◆

FINANCIAL security is one of the popular buzz phrases of the day.

You read it in scores of magazine and newspaper articles; you hear it on the lips of financial professionals and laypeople alike. And pretty soon the words come tumbling out of your own mouth: "Financial security. Yes. That's what I want."

It's an easy goal to embrace. After all, no one in his or her right mind would prefer financial *in*security.

But making financial security a priority is just the first—and easiest—step. Achieving it is harder. The task is complicated by an abundance of views on the subject. Everywhere you turn, there's another opinion:

Your broker says financial security is achieved by building a broad portfolio of stocks. Your banker argues that fixed-return investments are the ticket. Your insurance agent recommends a mind-numbing array of insurance policies.

Who is right? None of them and all of them, because financial security is a concept as individual as, well, each one of us.

What an advertising executive in New York needs to feel secure will be very different from what a teacher in Lansing, Michigan, feels he or she needs. Neither, however, will achieve that sense of security without a clear vision of his or her particular goals and a well-thought-out plan for achieving them.

What is it that makes *you* feel financially secure? Is it owning a home? Gold? Your own business? Is it being able to save steadily, pay bills regularly and fully, or have investment income flowing in? Is it as benign as having a good job, or as emotion-charged as having enough cash in the bank to cover a serious medical emergency?

Once you've pinpointed your feelings about financial security, the next step is to go after it! In Part One we explore how people with five separate views of financial security have done just that. You'll find inspiration and useful strategies here.

So much for the subjective side—what makes you *feel* secure. But true financial security goes beyond emotions to a sound financial plan, one that equips you to handle important planned events—the purchase of a new home, for example, as well as unexpected ones, like a career reversal or sudden illness.

Because the building blocks of financial security change as your life changes, we've created a step-by-step guide in Part Two that will help you chart a course of financial security at every significant stage of your adult life.

And for in-depth information on the tools you need to implement your financial security plan, turn to Part Three. You'll find tips on enhancing your income, protecting it in the case of disability, managing savings and investments, building a sound retirement plan, and much more.

Financial security is a road to be traveled as well as a destination. It's within your reach. The goal of this book is to help you achieve it safely and profitably.

*F*inancial *S*ecurity: *A V*ery *P*ersonal *M*atter

PEOPLE'S feelings about financial security run the gamut, from a Los Angeles art director who believes that financial security is "purely a state of mind," to a manager in a major New York corporation whose view is considerably more concrete: "I think who you're working for and the employee benefits offered determine financial security."

Clearly, financial security is, in part, a matter of personal opinion. However, in researching this book, we found that five views were voiced again and again, and we've explored them here.

This section is for you if your sense of financial security centers around: your home; investing your money for ultimate safety; being protected against inflation or other economic woes; being in complete control—as the boss of your own business; or being able to meet all your debt obligations on a regular basis.

Financial Security = Owning a Home ◆◆◆◆

"HOME is the center of my financial and emotional security," says June A. Ventura, an Arlington, Virginia, business executive.

Ventura speaks for hundreds of thousands of others for whom home ownership represents the ultimate security blanket, as well as the fulfillment of the American dream.

But Ventura adds a new twist: She's given up the notion of paying off her mortgage and owning the home free and clear. Though achieving that goal might make her breathe easier, maintaining the mortgage and tapping the equity in her home is a smarter move, she realizes. By taking out a home equity loan, she has gained access to some of the cash that otherwise would remain frozen in her home until it was sold. "My husband and I could probably pay off the mortgage now, but it just doesn't make sense," she explains, citing lost mortgage-interest tax deductions and the opportunity costs of locking cash in a non-income-producing asset as deterrents to the payoff strategy.

For full details on home equity loans and how you can use them to bolster your financial security, read on.

PUTTING YOUR HOME ON THE LINE (OF CREDIT)

If you're a homeowner with a paid-down mortgage, hefty equity, and a skimpy checking account balance, the ads in your newspaper look tempting:

THROW AWAY YOUR CREDIT CARDS!

TURN THE EQUITY IN YOUR HOME INTO CASH RESERVES!

These luring words are touting a relatively new concept in home equity loans that provides a line of credit with few, if any, strings on how you spend it, just like a bank credit card. Only the stakes are higher . . . and linked to a lien on your home.

While the familiar bank card—Master Card or Visa—may put $5,000 or $6,000 of buying power in your checkbook, these home equity loans bump your spending limits into the small-fortune category; $50,000, $100,000, $200,000, and even more, depending on your home's market value and on your ability to repay.

Those are big bucks, indeed; they offer you a chance to cash in on your home without selling out.

Should you go after them? Should you borrow against your home to raise cash for other spending?

The answer will depend on your circumstances, your self-discipline in handling money, and your comfort level when it comes to increasing the debt on your family's shelter.

If you look forward to the day you "burn the mortgage," or are one who considers a paid-for home central to financial security, then you're probably better off ignoring these financial blandishments and looking for cash elsewhere.

Some professional money managers, however, who tend to view bottom-line dollars in a dispassionate way, argue that a "frozen asset," such as equity in a home, should be made to work harder for its owner. Home equity is the difference between what you owe on your mortgage and the amount of cash you would have if you sold the house.

If you're like most people, home equity is the largest single asset you now hold—perhaps ever will—and one that grows every time you make a mortgage payment, or inflation or other economic factors nudge home values up another notch.

Unfortunately, home equity is also illiquid. It makes you rich on paper but doesn't enhance your cash flow, pay college or dentist bills, or improve your standard of living.

Unlike stocks and bonds, mutual fund shares, or investment real estate, your home equity earns no income. To tap it, you have only two choices: Sell the home, or borrow against it.

Home equity loans generally take two forms: (1) amortized/fixed payments; and (2) line of credit. Both are secured by liens against your personal home.

Amortized second mortgage. Familiar to almost anyone who owns real estate, this type of loan has been available virtually as long as first mortgages and is similar in structure. It normally has a fixed interest rate and a predetermined repayment period. You know from the start exactly what your monthly payments will be and how many you will have to make before the loan is paid. Further, you draw all the loan funds in one lump sum. Traditionally, amortized second mortgages carry higher interest rates and shorter repayment schedules than first mortgages.

Line of credit or cash reserve equity loans. These interesting financial devices offer the flexibility of bank-card financing but with much higher credit limits. The major feature of a cash reserve account is that, once established, you can borrow against it and repay at will. Further, you pay interest only on the money in use. While specific terms and conditions may differ slightly from one lender to another, all have several features in common:

◆ Your credit line is based on the equity in your home and on your ability to repay. Thus, a house worth $150,000 with a first mortgage of $50,000 might qualify for a $70,000 line of credit ($150,000 times 80 percent maximum loan exposure minus $50,000). A lender usually will allow you to borrow 50 to 80 percent of the amount of your home equity.

◆ All have floating interest rates evaluated quarterly and pegged to some agreed-upon financial benchmark—typically, 1 or 2 percent over the prevailing prime rate or the market quote on U.S. Treasury bills. Since the equity in your home is good collateral, banks will charge you these lower interest rates compared to "personal" and credit-card loans.

◆ You may draw funds only as you need them and pay interest only on funds you use. Most lenders, however, require fairly sizable drawdowns to rule out the account's use as a household checking device.

◆ Originating fees are relatively small, compared to those incurred in arranging conventional mortgage financing. You will be charged for an up-to-date appraisal, recording fees, and, likely, an annual management fee of thirty to fifty dollars. Some lenders charge points up front, but most don't.

◆ You have the option of paying only on the interest owed each month or of making voluntary principal payments as well.

Since interest rates fluctuate, as can the amount you owe, your monthly payments will vary, too. The good news is that you will not suffer negative amortization. Conversely, in times of rapidly rising interest rates, your monthly bill could increase alarmingly.

Ticking off all the features, you might almost believe these flexible home equity loans are sensational:

◆ You need not sell your home to tap its equity, a considerable plus if you're fortunate enough to be sitting on a low-interest first mortgage, you want to keep the home, or economic conditions have driven buyers out of the marketplace.

◆ Flexibility has to be rated a plus, too. You have credit available when you need it without repeated application costs. And you have the freedom to dip into the loan only when the need arises.

◆ Money loaned against equity is tax-free. It allows you to tap your illiquid asset without paying capital gains tax. And the interest you pay to borrow the funds probably will be tax-deductible.

◆ You'll almost surely repay the funds you use with cheaper dollars. Though inflation has calmed considerably from its virulent double-digit days, it still continues.

◆ You are borrowing against an *appreciating* asset. While exceptions may exist, chances are great that your equity will continue to grow through the forces of principal paydown and inflationary and other economic pressures.

What, then, are the pitfalls?

◆ Under 1986 tax reform legislation, interest deductions will be allowed only for loans in the amount of the original purchase price of the home plus improvements. Homeowners who wish to take out loans for the *appreciated value* of their homes will lose much of the interest deduction; the restriction will be phased in over four years beginning in 1987. The only exceptions are for borrowers who use loan proceeds for educational tuition or medical expenses.

◆ Fluctuating interest rates mean monthly payments that can increase rapidly in short order. If you want to hang on to your home, you should make sure your budget can cover increased interest costs . . . and principal paydown—even when you haven't borrowed additional money.

◆ Should you have to sell your home in a severe economic downturn, you may have to settle for less than your combined mortgages. That means you may have to come up with cash or tap other assets to clear the debt.

◆ You must also be on guard against readily available credit dulling your sense of value. Access to huge sums via the simple expedient of writing a check may make you a complacent shopper—who fails to seek out the best value or the cheapest source of funds.

And finally, a large line of credit capacity secured by your home may shut out your chances of obtaining other, cheaper loans—even when your credit line is untapped.

Why? Because all the credit at your disposal pushes your potential debt toward its upper capacity.

The situation may cause you problems if you are seeking special-purpose credit. A car loan, for instance, at this writing, is 2 to 4 percent cheaper than a home equity loan line of credit; it's a far better value for the smart financial manager. Your banker may well refuse your application because he or she perceives you as having too much available credit, even though you are not using it and don't intend to.

In another scenario, perhaps you want the funds to acquire income-producing property, certainly an excellent use of credit. Yet, by shrewd shopping, you may be able to accomplish your purpose through cheaper owner financing or by diligently seeking low down-payment deals.

You should also be wary of letting readily available funds blur your investment judgment. Using borrowed money to plunge on a "hot" stock tip is loaded with peril. *The trick is to make sure the projected return on your investment will be greater than your borrowing costs.* And whether you use it to buy income-producing real estate, make other investments, or start a new business, assess your odds for success carefully.

Some lenders insist you sign a statement certifying that loan proceeds will *not* be used for purchasing securities. Some state laws, too, carry restrictions on the use of home equity loan funds.

Dr. Peter Kares, chairman of the finance department of the University of South Florida, advises caution: "Anytime you increase your debt, you're increasing your risks." While he agrees that a home equity loan can be enormously valuable to the prudent investor, he also maintains that such a device is only one route to investable cash. "There are lots of ways to raise money for investments or other personal needs, and a home equity loan is just one alternative. There might be a cheaper way," he says.

In the final analysis, only you can decide if a home equity loan makes sense for you.

HOW HOME EQUITY LOANS BUILD FINANCIAL SECURITY

The wisdom of borrowing money against the equity in your home will surely depend on your emotional comfort with added debt, but even more importantly, on your ability to use the money to improve your financial statement. Here are some ideas that may work for you:

Increase retirement savings. The 1986 Tax Reform Act added some wrinkles to IRA eligibility. The upshot is that you are still entitled to shelter $2,000 per wage earner in a tax-free IRA if you're not covered by an employer plan and your joint adjusted gross income is less than $40,000, or $25,000 on a single return. The deduction is phased out for joint filers with adjusted gross income over $40,000 but under $50,000, and $25,000 to $35,000 for singles. As before, an additional $250 may be invested for a nonworking spouse. Interest, dividends, and other income and capital gains distributions earned by your IRA continue tax-deferred despite other 1986 tax law changes. The magic of IRAs' nontaxable compounding means that the earlier you make your contributions each year into fixed-interest investments, the higher your ultimate yield will be. An equity loan can make the funds available to you on January 1, if you wish. And you can write the interest charges off on your income tax.

Buy income-producing real estate. Dividing equity among a home and other real estate holdings will usually produce a stronger financial statement than will ownership of a single property. For example, split $50,000 equity between a home valued at $100,000 and a small apartment building worth $100,000, and you have effective control of $200,000 in real estate. The same cash locked into a home alone means you control only $100,000 worth of assets. Furthermore, addition of the income property to your portfolio positions you for additional tax savings, cash flow, and later on, capital gains.

Buy a second home. You may be eyeing a vacation villa at your favorite resort and command enough income to justify its purchase. An equity loan on your principal residence may be the smart way to finance your dream.

Swing a bridge loan. As its name implies, a bridge loan spans the gap between an old mortgage and a new one. You may find it useful if you are in the process of selling your present home and, at the same time, buying or building a new one. Bridge funds buy short-term time, allowing you temporarily to finance two homes at once.

Enhance the salability of your home. Many home equity loans can be assumed (with permission of the lender) by a new owner. Thus, merged with an existing first mortgage into a new financial package, the home equity loan has the potential to make your property affordable to a wider spectrum of cash-poor buyers. They'll be able to buy with less money up front.

TURN YOUR HOME INTO A CASH MACHINE

In addition to home equity loans, there are at least nine other ways to turn your home into an income generator and a greater source of financial security than ever before.

1. Do business from home. Whether you operate your own business full-time, work for someone else, or moonlight, a home office can yield excellent returns on your home investment if you set it up correctly.

Operating costs are only part of the story. You can also figure auto expenses beginning at your driveway, rather than from your first stop, as with other businesses.

Putting your children to work in your own business offers another family benefit. Tax rules allow you to pay them a salary, assuming it is reasonable for the work performed. Typically, the youngsters pay little or no tax, effectively increasing overall, after-tax income for the family.

CAUTION: Check whether your business must be registered with the state or local government and if there are any zoning regulations for your residential area. Also check your homeowner's insurance policies carefully. Make sure your liability coverage includes "business invitees." And bear in mind you'll have to pay self-employment business taxes.

2. Become a dealer for manufactured housing. Your home can double as a demonstrator model as well as shelter for your family. Manufactured housing (not to be confused with so-called prefabs) is capturing an increasingly larger share of the quality housing market, and you may find a style that suits your family.

Nancy and Gary Marquis, for example, built their demonstrator home northwest of Gainesville, Florida, and became the Florida dealer for the manufacturer of New England Log Homes.

Though the home is used for business, it also houses the family, so they can't write off any home-operating costs beyond the normal mortgage interest charges and real-estate taxes. However, substantial earnings from every home they sell (10 to 15 percent of an average $20,000 sale) make the dealership a profitable arrangement for them.

CAUTION: Examine your family's habits before committing yourselves to having strangers tramp through on a moment's notice. Also investigate the history, stability, and quality of the company you're thinking of representing.

3. Start a bed-and-breakfast hostelry. The B and B, which originated in Europe, calls for housing travelers in private homes and serving just the first meal of the day. George and Barbara Klein are doing that with their home in Croton-on-Hudson, New York, and grossing over $20,000 a year.

For the Kleins, it started because their big, old Victorian house, built when energy was cheap, was consuming almost every cent its modern-day owners brought home. "We burned forty-three hundred gallons of fuel that first winter, and taxes ran sixty-two hundred dollars. At that point, we realized some hard decisions had to be made."

That prompted the birth of their bed-and-breakfast business. "We had the home for it, the location—and the desire for me to stay home with our baby we'd waited twelve years to have," Barbara says. The Kleins now keep three rooms available for guests fifty weeks a year. Barbara says vacationers are not the only customers. Many traveling businesspeople prefer the relatively low cost and comfortable atmosphere of a private home over an impersonal commercial hotel.

CAUTION: Check local zoning laws before joining a B and B network. New York State, for example, allows the housing of paying guests in private homes as long as there is no sign outside and fewer than ten persons are in residence on a daily basis. Specifics vary from state to state.

4. Conduct seminars or classes at home. If yours is a marketable skill others will pay to learn; consider holding classes at home. Not only can you save money on overhead, but you may pick up some tax savings. Gourmet cooking, needlepoint, fly tying, sculpture, architecture, investment know-how, photography—people are interested in an endless list of subjects.

Consider putting home amenities to work, too. For example, a pool if you have one. Can you teach toddlers to swim? Or older people who are too shy for public lessons?

CAUTION: Always check with your insurance agent about liability coverage before you bring outsiders into your home for business reasons.

5. Rent special-purpose facilities. Perhaps your home is equipped with a darkroom, thanks to your photography hobby. Or you have a basement full of woodworking tools. Consider letting others use them—for a fee.

6. Rent storage space. Look around your home for unused space. Perhaps an extra stall in the garage is just what the owner of a fancy sports car needs desperately. You may have extra attic or basement space begging to be partitioned and rented to an apartment dweller who inherited Grandma's dining-room set but, unfortunately, has nowhere to put it.

CAUTION: Make sure your tenant is insured against loss while the property is in your home.

7. Rent a room. Fill that empty upstairs bedroom with a college professor or student. Not only will it generate rental income and tax savings for you, but you'll have a resident "house sitter" when you leave home.

CAUTION: Agree on house rules with your prospective tenant *before* he or she moves in.

8. Sell off unwanted trees. If your property is heavily shaded, consider selling some of the trees. Not only will you create a sunny spot in your yard, but you may pick up enough money for serious investing. Southern landscapers are often on the lookout for healthy palms and will pay as much as $500 apiece for them. In northern sawmills, walnut and other hardwoods are in demand. Your vegetation can also be profitably harvested, including herbs and spices grown in your garden.

9. Swap space for services. Your home needs painting. You might cut the bill by exchanging storage space, inside or out, for labor.

CAUTION: Check with your tax advisor on how such barter income would be treated for tax purposes.

TAX STRATEGIES

Keep these points in mind in connection with the cash-generating ideas discussed above.

◆ A home office may be used for any trade or business you engage in. It doesn't have to be your principal line of work, but the space must be used exclusively for that purpose to qualify. For example, if you're a lawyer who runs a real estate business from home, you can deduct the relevant home-office expenses under "Miscellaneous Deductions" on your tax form. That would include a portion of costs for the entire home (such as utilities, insurance, general upkeep, and so on) and the total of any expenses that relate only to the business. However, under the 1986 Tax Reform Act, miscellaneous expenses are deductible only to the extent they exceed 2 percent of adjusted gross income.

◆ When you rent out all or part of your home:

. . . You must allocate expenses between deductible rental use and nondeductible personal use, much as you would in apportioning expenses for a home office. Again, any expenses incurred solely for the rental part (such as painting rented rooms, or the cost of extra liability insurance) are deductible in full.

. . . If you rent your home only during your two-week vacation, you don't have to report the rent you receive as income. So if there's an annual event in your area that attracts tourists, consider taking your family vacation then; the money you make on your home may pay for your trip. (CAUTION: If you rent your home for more than fifteen days, you must declare *all* rental income.)

. . . Any improvements you make for the sole use of rental units (say, a new kitchen or bath) should be specifically allocated to the rental part of the property and depreciated as such when you file your income taxes. This can also prove advantageous when you sell your house. The allocation of the total price of the improvement will raise the cost basis of the business portion of the property and consequently reduce your taxable gain.

. . . Renting your home can be especially beneficial tax-wise if you're planning to sell it and expect the sale to result in a loss. By renting it for a year or two, your otherwise nondeductible loss becomes deductible.

Financial Security = Investing Conservatively ◆◆◆◆

FOR investors who demand absolute certainty that every cent they invest will come back to them, with interest, there is really only one choice—securities of the federal government.

Treasury bills, notes, and bonds. Securities issued through the Treasury Department carry the full faith, credit, and taxing power of the United States government, which means that as long as our government continues, its obligations will be repaid.

Buying government securities essentially means lending money to Uncle Sam for anywhere from three months to more than ten years. The government offers investors a wide variety of securities to choose from.

The shortest-term obligations of the government are Treasury bills, also known as T-bills. They are issued with maturities of thirteen weeks (three months), twenty-six weeks (six months), and fifty-two weeks (one year). The minimum investment is $10,000.

T-bills are sold in book-entry form, meaning you receive receipts from the Treasury rather than certificates.

Next on the maturity scale are Treasury notes. Notes are considered medium-term obligations, carrying maturities from two to ten years.

For notes having maturities of four years or less, the minimum purchase price is $5,000, which can be increased in multiples of $1,000. Notes over four years carry minimums of $1,000.

Treasury bonds are the longest-term obligations of the government, with maturities extending beyond ten years. Treasury bonds occasionally are issued with a call provision, which means the government can redeem the bond (with interest, of course) before the maturity date.

Bonds, like notes, are issued in book-entry form. Bonds and notes issued before 1983 were sold in bearer form, meaning the securities could be redeemed by anyone presenting them for payment. These still may be bought on the open market from a brokerage firm or bank. The minimum purchase price of Treasury bonds is $1,000, which can be increased by multiples of $1,000.

Interest you earn on Treasury securities is exempt from state and local income taxes.

There is one other type of Treasury security worth mentioning—U.S. Savings Bonds. Series EE and Series HH U.S. Savings Bonds are a special type of Treasury bond. Series EE bonds are priced in varying amounts from $50 to $10,000. You buy them at half of face value and get no payments of either interest or principal until you redeem them. If you redeem EE bonds at any time during the first five years, you receive a fixed interest rate. If you do not redeem them during the first five years, the interest rate is adjusted every six months to equal 85 percent of the average rate on five-year Treasury notes. You are guaranteed at least 6 percent interest after the fifth year. You can redeem EE bonds for face value after twelve years. You pay no state or local tax and pay federal tax only when you cash them in.

Series HH bonds start at $500 face value and go up to $10,000. You cannot buy HH bonds for cash. You purchase them in exchange for Series EE or old Series E Savings Bonds— or with redemptive proceeds of old Series H bonds that have matured. When you get HH bonds you pay the full face value; they pay out interest twice a year instead of at redemption. You must pay federal tax on this interest each year, but it is exempt from state and local taxes. The current rate on HH bonds is 6 percent. You get your principal back when they mature in ten years.

Agency securities. In addition to the Treasury, many federal agencies also issue securities. Some of these are backed by the full faith and credit of the government, others by the issuing agency. No agency ever has defaulted, however, and most issues offer higher yields than Treasury obligations.

While dozens of agency securities are available, those most widely traded are from agencies that promote home ownership and agriculture.

The twelve Federal Home Loan Banks (FHLBs), the organizations that advance home mortgage credit to the nation's thrift institutions, are among the most active agency issuers.

FHLB securities include notes with maturities of under one year and bonds with maturities of up to ten years. They are not guaranteed by the government, but are backed by mortgages, cash, and Treasury securities. Minimum purchase requirement is $10,000, and interest income, while subject to federal income tax, is exempt from state and local income tax.

The Federal National Mortgage Association (FNMA), or Fannie Mae, is another large issuer. Federally chartered but publicly owned (FNMA shares are traded on the New York Stock Exchange), Fannie Mae buys residential mortgages from banks and thrifts in order to provide liquidity in the nation's mortgage markets. Fannie Mae securities are not guaranteed by the government and are subject to all taxes. The certificates are guaranteed by Fannie Mae and are available in bearer form in minimum denominations of $1,000, with a maturity of approximately fifteen to thirty years.

Other mortgage-backed securities include those issued by the Government National Mortgage Association (Ginnie Mae) and the Federal Home Loan Mortgage Corporation (Freddie Mac). These agencies' securities may be bought from securities firms; minimum purchase is $25,000.

You also can buy mutual funds that specialize in government mortgage-backed securities. This way you can invest smaller amounts and obtain an interest in a diversified portfolio professionally managed.

Agriculture-related issuers include the Farmers Home Administration and the Federal Farm Credit Consolidated System. The International Bank for Reconstruction and Development (at the World Bank), the Maritime Administration, the Small Business Administration, the Tennessee Valley Authority (TVA), and the U.S. Postal Service also issue securities, which may be obtained through securities firms.

How to buy government securities. Treasury bills may be purchased without a service charge from the U.S. Treasury in Washington, or at any of the twelve Federal Reserve regional banks or their twenty-five branches. Commercial banks and securities firms will purchase T-bills for their customers for a fee.

Merrill Lynch, for example, charges customers a commission of fifty dollars to buy a T-bill, as does Chase Manhattan Bank. Charles Schwab and Company, a discount broker, charges twenty dollars.

To purchase T-bills directly, you must submit a tender requesting purchase by mail or in person to a Federal Reserve bank or branch. Federal Reserve Regional banks are located in New York City, Boston, Philadelphia, Cleveland, Richmond, Atlanta, Chicago, St. Louis, Minneapolis, Kansas City, Dallas, and San Franciso. You are required to indicate whether you want to bid competitively or noncompetitively. Competitive bidders—banks and other professional buyers—name the exact price they wish to pay. But you, as an individual investor, should check the "Noncompetitive Bid" box, indicating you will pay the average of the competitive bids accepted by the Treasury.

T-bill auctions are held frequently. The thirteen-week and twenty-six-week bills are offered each week. Public announcement—usually in the business section of major newspapers—is made every Tuesday, with the auction on the following Monday. The bills are issued on Thursday, three days after the auction.

One-year T-bills are issued every four weeks. The offering is announced every fourth Thursday, with the auction taking place the following Thursday. The bills are issued a week later, on the next Thursday. Auction schedules are modified when either the announcement, auction, or issue date falls on a holiday.

In addition to the tender, you must submit a certified or bank check (or matured Treasury securities) for the full face amount of the T-bills to be purchased. After the Treasury receives a tender and holds an auction, it will send you a check for the difference between the face amount of the T-bill and the auction price. This is the discount, and it represents the return on your investment. At maturity, the Treasury will deposit a check representing the face value of the T-bill into an account specified by you. If you choose, however, the Treasury may roll over the proceeds into another T-bill. You then will receive another check for the discount on the new purchase.

The process for purchasing Treasury notes and bonds is similar to that for T-bills.

Treasury securities—bills, notes, and bonds—also may be acquired indirectly through the purchase of shares in mutual funds that specialize in Treasury securities.

Two useful guides to the Treasury market, which include information helpful in filling out the necessary forms, are *Buying Treasury Securities at Federal Reserve Banks,* free from the Federal Reserve Bank of Richmond (Public Services Department, P.O. Box 27622, Richmond, Virginia 23261), and *The Dow Jones-Irwin Guide to Buying and Selling Treasury Securities,* by Howard M. Berlin (Dow Jones-Irwin, 1820 Ridge Road, Homewood, Illinois 60430).

The pros and cons. Government securities offer you a number of pluses:

◆ *Safety of principal and interest.* The United States government guarantees full repayment of principal at maturity.

Agencies whose securities are not backed by the government are usually able to draw on the Treasury in emergencies.

◆ *Yield.* The return on most government securities is competitive with other investment yields.

◆ *Liquidity.* There is an active secondary market for government securities, meaning that you can sell your holdings at any time before the maturity date. Prices on the open market fluctuate with prevailing interest rates, however, so that you may receive less by selling it early than you will if you hold on to the bond until maturity.

◆ *Noncallable issues.* Most government securities cannot be called before maturity. This means you, as owner, are guaranteed a stated amount of interest for the entire life of the security.

◆ *Flexibility.* The wide range of maturities of government securities permits you to match your objectives more easily than with other types of investments.

While government securities offer several advantages, chief among the potential risks is that of rising interest rates. The yawning federal deficit has so increased the government's financing needs that new issues may have to be sold at higher rates to attract sufficient funds. If so, the higher returns of new issues would tend to depress the value of existing securities, since the older ones pay lower rates of interest.

Financial Security = Owning Gold

AN artist who says that sometimes she barely has enough money to pay the bills has owned a gold bar for many years.

"I've had times when I really should have traded it in to get over rough spots, but I think of it as ultimate security. I would use it if I were starving."

A man who has just come into a sizable inheritance says he is worried about money now—for the first time in his life.

"I have a lawyer and an investment advisor," he says, "and they've given me good advice. But I'm worried that we're going to have another depression and I'll lose everything. I've been buying gold bars and putting them in a safe place. If the worst happens, I'll have something to fall back on."

There seems to be more emotion attached to owning gold than to other types of investments. And people who look to it for their financial security often have lived through a devastating period of economic inflation, depression, or personal loss.

THE GOLDEN RULES

As an investment, gold is volatile. It generally increases in value as the value of paper money shrinks, so it has traditionally been held as a hedge against inflation. Should you be drawn to gold as an emotional or real investment in financial security, know that certain forms of gold are more profitable than others, and certain forms are more trouble than they are worth.

Here are the ways you can own it:

Jewelry. The purity of gold is measured in karats, in fractions of 24-karat (pure) old. Since pure gold is usually considered too soft, most jewelry comes in 14K or 18K of fineness, alloyed with copper, silver, nickel, or zinc to reduce malleability. The price of gold jewelry is determined not only by gold content, but by factors such as design, workmanship, and retail markup. Compared to other forms of gold, jewelry can be purchased at little cost. Changing fashion and high retail markup make jewelry a relatively poor investment compared to other options, although there is a strong market for antique and other rare gold jewelry items.

Coins. There are but two types of gold coins—bullion coins and numismatic coins. The value of bullion coins lies in their gold content. Numismatic coins (collectors' specialties) are valued by both their bullion content and their rarity.

The most actively traded bullion coins are the South African Krugerrand, the Canadian Maple Leaf, the Mexican 50 peso, and the American Eagle. The advantages of buying bullion coins are: They come in small denominations, so are easily accessible to small investors; they're easy to store; purity is guaranteed; and they're easily bought and sold through precious-metals dealers, coin shops, and brokerage firms. It takes little expertise to invest in them, and coins don't have to be assayed (to confirm their content or metal weight) when they're sold.

Numismatic coins can be just as, or more, profitable than other forms of gold ownership, but require buyers to have a certain level of expertise, or expert guidance, in choosing the right investment.

Gold bullion bars. Bars come in sizes up to 400 ounces. If you decide to take possession, you can buy as little as a 1-ounce bar, but you must pay for shipment and insurance, and must have the bar assayed before reselling it.

Gold certificates. An alternative to taking physical possession is to buy a gold certificate, which is basically a receipt stating how much gold you own and where it is stored. Minimum investment for a certificate can be as low as $1,000. You will have to pay for storage (in a depository bank either here or abroad) and insurance, but you eliminate the problems of shipment and assaying. This is one type of investment where it's absolutely essential to deal with a reputable broker.

Gold mining stocks. Stocks, primarily of Canadian, American, and South African companies, are traded on the various stock exchanges or over-the-counter like any other issue. This type of investment is more speculative than owning gold itself, partly because of political considerations, and partly because of the high cost of mining. There also are gold processing stocks.

Gold-based mutual funds. There are a variety of gold and precious metals funds to choose from, and many have minimum initial investments as low as $500. Some funds invest in bullion, some in gold mining/processing stocks, some in both, and others combine investments in gold with investments in other precious metals. Some concentrate on companies located in a specific region, such as North America. The fund's prospectus will list all investments, so you'll be able to assess if what they're holding is approximately what you want to invest in. The combination of professional management, diversified holdings, low initial and subsequent investment amounts, convenience and liquidity makes this an attractive way for small investors to own gold. You can check comparative performances of funds you're considering in the periodic surveys of *Barron's, Forbes, Business Week, Sylvia Porter's Personal Finance Magazine,* and other publications.

Gold futures and forwards. Hang on for a great (or disastrous) ride with these. They are the most speculative forms of investment, suitable only for sophisticated investors. With gold futures, investors buy or sell contracts on a certain amount of gold at a certain price at a certain point in the future. Gold forwards work the same way, except that you can call in your investment at any time within a given period (up to eighteen months). Futures and forwards give investors leverage: They can control a larger share of the market than they would have with direct purchases—by only having to put up a part of the purchase price and borrowing the balance from the broker.

You also can buy futures on silver, platinum, and palladium. There also are commodity funds (also known as pools, many of which are limited partnerships) that buy and sell futures, in which you can invest.

Gold stock options. Another speculative approach is trading in options on the stocks or on indexes of stocks of companies engaged in gold (and precious metals and minerals) operations, such as mining, processing, services, and manufactured products.

Whether you want to own gold for the financial security you feel it brings, or for its sheer beauty alone, make sure you research your purchase carefully—not only for its investment value, but for the reputation of the dealer you are buying it from. Beware especially of telephone salespeople who try to pressure you into a quick and expensive purchase. A call to your local Better Business Bureau may prevent you from making a costly mistake.

Financial Security = Being My Own Boss ♦♦♦♦

PEOPLE are discovering that the corporate nest is not so comfortably feathered these days:

Once-benevolent employers, who lavished loyal workers with liberal benefits and overtime pay have—in many cases—given way to heartless counterparts, who lay off employees, shut down plants, order pay cutbacks, and usher managers out the early retirement door.

As the corporate ship sinks, more and more survivors are climbing aboard the "S.S. Entrepreneur," seeking greater career and financial security than they left behind.

There's a certain irony here, since starting a business is one of the riskiest ventures around: 50 percent of new, small businesses fail within the first four years of operation, according to the Small Business Administration.

Still, for those scathed by the corporate wars, and anyone who considers "being in control" the key to security, entrepreneurship holds a powerful appeal.

In addition, it offers attractive financial planning benefits which—if well utilized—can add measurably to your financial security. And you needn't forsake the corporate nest altogether to take advantage of them. Sideline entrepreneurs have equal access to these useful strategies.

TAX SAVINGS

To start with, tax deductions generated by your business can be used to offset investment or retirement income, as well as the income you earn as an employee if you're launching your business as a sideline operation. That sets your business apart from passive tax shelters such as real estate limited partnerships, whose losses under the Tax Reform Act of 1986 can no longer be handled this way.

Another tax strategy available to entrepreneurs is hiring family members—the only form of income shifting still viable after tax reform. The strategy works like this: Hire your children, pay them a fair and reasonable wage for the duties they perform, then deduct these wages as a business expense. Another benefit: Income your children earn is tax-free so long as each child's total earnings do not exceed $2,540 (in 1987).

By going into business you will also be able to write off in full many miscellaneous expenses now off-limits to employees, unless they exceed 2 percent of adjusted gross income. These "miscellaneous deductions" include such things as business journals, continuing-education courses, union or professional dues, and business-related travel.

Now that consumer interest deductions have been curtailed, savvy entrepreneurs have an additional edge over employees: They can turn personal interest payments into business interest, which remains deductible under the new law. An example: Designate one of the family cars—the one with the big loan on it—as a company car. Interest can then be written off to the extent you use the car for business.

RETIREMENT PLANNING FLEXIBILITY

As a self-employed person, you may establish and contribute to a tax-favored Keogh or Simplified Employee Pension (SEP-IRA) retirment plan. Both plans offer greater personal control and more liberal funding allowances than retirement plans available to you as an employee. Tax reform has curbed tax-deductible contributions to IRAs, and capped employee 401(k) retirement plan contributions at $7,000 a year. Earnings on

IRA and 401(k) contributions are tax-deferred until withdrawn. These earnings may include interest, dividends, and capital-gains distributions. With these curbs on IRAs and 401(k)s the flexible retirement plans of the self-employed look more appealing than ever.

Both Keoghs and SEP-IRAs are tax-deductible and tax-deferred plans. A business owner may shelter as much as 25 percent of earned income, to a maximum $30,000, in a Keogh, or a maximum 15 percent of earned income, up to $30,000, in a SEP. Since the self-employed may only contribute to one of these plans in a tax year, it's important to consider four major differences before making your choice:

The first is obvious: If you want to stash away as much profit as possible, the Keogh allows you to shelter the higher maximum percentage.

But if simplification is your major concern, you may want to opt for the SEP-IRA. The start-up form and plan description are short and simple, and the IRS requires no separate reporting forms. In fact, you don't need a custodian's plan prototype as you do with a Keogh; the IRS will send you Form 5305-SEP. With a Keogh plan, however, you're likely to want both a money purchase plan and a profit-sharing plan, for maximum flexibility and money-saving potential. Each plan requires a separate setup and IRS reporting form. If you are the sole proprietor and participant in your Keogh plan, yearly reports to the IRS are made using the relatively short 5500R forms. But if you employ even one worker, you'll have to file the byzantine 5500C (and refile it every three years, unless you opt to switch over to the 5500R form in your fourth year), which usually demands the skills of a tax advisor. Because many accountants are unfamiliar with this form, the bill for time spent completing it may mean added expense in maintaining your retirement plan. Some plan custodians offer telephone assistance to clients in completing Keogh forms, a possibility worth investigating when setting up your plan.

If you are paperwork phobic, you can easily roll over a cumbersome Keogh into a SEP-IRA. But that step will be final; the IRS won't let you go the other way—rolling a SEP into a Keogh.

A third consideration: Though, as a general rule, the new tax law eliminates income averaging, a few exceptions apply to Keogh holders: Those who turned 50 before January 1, 1986, may use five- or ten-year income averaging on a one-time-only basis when they begin to take their retirement plan distribution (after age 59½). Those who turned 59½ before January 1, 1987, are eligible for five-year income averaging on a one-time-only basis.

In contrast, your SEP-IRA payout does not qualify for this favorable tax treatment at all.

Finally, if you have employees in your business, or if you may in the future, there are critical points to consider in choosing between a Keogh or a SEP-IRA. A Keogh plan will allow you to keep more income for yourself, if that's your primary goal. The SEP-IRA requires you to make contributions for any employee twenty-one years or older who has rendered *any* service during three of the past five years. That includes any work performed for any period of time, not necessarily consecutive, for at least $300 in annual wages. By contrast, under a Keogh plan you are required to provide for employees twenty-one or older with two years' service (the plan may specify consecutive service), of at least 1,000 hours in a year. If there is a chance you'll ever hire employees, know that even a part-time worker will have to be included under a SEP-IRA. This can be a very negative feature for the person who sets up this plan to maximize individual savings from profits.

On the other hand, perhaps the success of your enterprise depends on attracting and keeping good employees. The Keogh can work to your advantage in that case, because graduated vesting in the plan can begin after just one year of service.

Financial Security = Being Able to Pay the Bills ◆◆◆

"MY idea of financial security is being able to pay my bills," says Jenny Cooke, a Portland, Oregon, attorney. What lies behind Cooke's adamant statement is a spiraling series of events that plunged her and husband, Edward Jones, also an attorney, into serious financial difficulty. Their story and comments may ring some bells with you:

"To be honest," says Cooke, "I never thought we'd be the type to fall seriously into debt but, in retrospect, it's not hard to see how it happened."

In a period of a year the couple bought an $82,000 home, had a baby, and became a one-income family as Cooke gave up her private law practice to devote time to their new son.

In the wake of these sweeping changes, the couple toted up $5,000 in delinquent bills owed to a total of twenty creditors. "We were getting threatening letters and phone calls," Jones recalls. "Some of our creditors were ready to sue us." Says Jenny, "It got to the point where I hated to pick up the phone."

Have you been there? If so, you can appreciate how important the ability to stay on top of debts can be.

Debt problems cut across all economic lines and age groups. No one is immune. A medical emergency or serious illness can be the trigger. So can a layoff, firing, or divorce. An almost imperceptible rise in personal expenses is another common culprit.

The menace of today's easy-credit society is that it's not always apparent when bills are getting out of hand. With countless lines of credit available to you, it becomes possible to have an extravagant life-style while you sink deeper and deeper into the black hole of debt.

Staying attuned to financial limits during periods of personal or family crisis is unquestionably a struggle, as well. Often, in an effort to keep emotional equilibrium, you overspend and lose that struggle.

THE EARLY WARNING SIGNS OF DEBT

By learning to recognize, unmistakably, when you're approaching the brink of financial overextension, you can head off serious credit problems and stay in control of your debts.

Here are the tip-offs:

◆ You are borrowing to the hilt of your credit limits.
◆ Your charge and bank-card balances are rising each month, and you're just barely making the minimum monthly payments on them.
◆ You are dipping into savings to meet normal household expenses, and using credit for these essentials.
◆ You are falling behind on critical monthly payments, such as rent, mortgage, or a car loan.
◆ You are using one form of credit (a bank-card cash advance, for example) to make payments on other credit debt.
◆ You are vaguely aware of your monthly payments, but you are unable to name all your creditors and the total amount you owe them.
◆ You are spending 20 percent or more of your yearly take-home pay on installment debt (exclusive of your home mortgage).

The 20 percent figure is a guideline that's been commonly used as an outer limit. But Virginia Nagel, executive vice president of Consumer Credit Counseling Services of St. Louis, counsels, "To be safe, it's better to *spend no more than fifteen percent of your after-tax pay.*" Other experts disagree. "Fifteen or twenty years ago this twenty percent figure made sense. But today, after bouts of inflation and recession, it's usually too low," says one family financial counselor. Indeed, at today's prices, if you're going to stick to this rule, those buying a car must automatically exclude themselves from having other credit, which means paying cash for all other purchases—a herculean task for many growing families.

If you do apply the 20 percent guideline to your own situation, remember: It is *only* a guideline, not a hard-and-fast rule. If your take-home pay is low, or you have high expenses for basics, spending 20 percent of your net pay on installment debt may be too much. But if your take-home pay is relatively high and you have low expenses for necessities you can probably afford to take on more installment debt than the 20 percent guideline allows.

If you recognize your own situation in the warning signs above, or if you are receiving dunning notices from your creditors, how can you start reducing your debt overload *now*?

GETTING BACK IN THE BLACK

Contact *all* your creditors immedately. Do not avoid their calls and letters; this is the worst possible strategy. Almost everyone falls behind in payments at some time in life; creditors know this. They would much rather accept reduced payments from you than be forced to repossess your car, for example, or take legal action.

When you contact them, your creditors will want to know why you cannot make your payments (be honest), and what reduced payments will be affordable to you.

To answer the latter, a thorough assessment of your annual income and outgo must be made. If the very idea of this task overwhelms you, relax. Expert credit counseling services are available to you free or at low cost (see page 44). Whether you prefer to go it alone, or enlist a credit counselor's assistance, here is the range of solutions to free up money to repay your debts. Which one(s) you choose will depend on you and your family's unique situation, values, and temperament.

Decreasing expenses. First look for the reductions that cause the least disruption in your life-style. For example, recreational expenses can usually be pared down substantially. Of course, the deeper your indebtedness, the more dramatic the reductions you must make in your expenses.

Restructuring current debt. Your options include negotiating reduced payment schedules on revolving credit debt and asking creditors to rewrite the terms of a loan contract or mortgage. Once new terms have been agreed to, it's critical that you adhere to them religiously.

In most cases, restructured credit arrangements appear on your credit rating as delinquencies, even though your creditors have agreed to lower payments. To ensure that your *future* creditors do not misinterpret these delinquencies, exercise your right to include a one-hundred-word statement in your credit history explaining the circumstances of your restructured debt.

Consolidating your loans. Extend the term of your indebtedness while reducing numerous bills to one manageable monthly payment. Take care to secure a reasonable rate of interest on your loan so your overall indebtedness does not skyrocket.

Liquidating assets. Can you part with one of the family cars, or sell a little-loved, but valuable heirloom? Check the attic, basement, and your investment records for forgotten assets that are worth cashing in.

Bankruptcy. There is no formula for determining when your debt has reached a level where bankruptcy is the best route for you. And there is no getting around the fact that bankruptcy is an extremely serious step, with long-term repercussions.

PREVENTING DEBT OVERLOAD

Once the crisis has passed, there are a few strategies you can employ for sound debt management.

The first and most fundamental: *Reform your financial perspective from a short- to a long-term outlook.*

Plan your debt. Be aware of fixed, cyclical expenses, and prepare for them. Add up all your expenditures for the past year or several years (this means reviewing your records: receipts, income tax forms, check stubs, *everything*) to get a fair idea of your average annual outlay. Compare this figure to your yearly take-home pay. If your expenses are edging up too closely on your income, it will be evident. Also evident will be the sources of any excessive cash drains.

Institute quarterly or (ideally) monthly family financial conferences. At these sessions, family members (including youngsters, if they have reached an age where they can understand) review the family's current expenses and income. Short- and long-term goals are set (in six months a new car, in a year a family vacation) and everyone has a say. These conferences are ideal for teaching children about money management. "Kids come to understand priorities—the difference between a want and a need. They learn that money is finite, and pick up valuable budgeting habits," explains Edward Roach, director of Consumer Credit Counseling at the Greensboro, North Carolina, Family and Children's Services Association. Equally important, by allowing all family members to participate in decision making, tensions and resentments about financial sacrifices are lessened. "The conferences reduce the likelihood of budget-busting behavior, and give the whole family a vision into the future," says Roach. "This farsightedness is critical, because the longer the time frame people have financially, the more financially stable they will be."

CONSUMER CREDIT COUNSELING SERVICES

A credit counseling agency will hope you work out a sound budget, determine equitable payments to each of your creditors, and negotiate with your creditors on your behalf, if you wish. An initial session requires roughly a two-hour time commitment. Follow-up is generally conducted over the phone. Information you reveal is held in confidence, and the services are free or available for a nominal fee—that is, if you are dealing with a nonprofit agency. Some of the best nonprofits are:

◆ The National Foundation for Consumer Credit. For a free listing of counseling centers in your area write: NFCC, 8701 Georgia Avenue, Silver Spring, Maryland 20910.

◆ Family Service America (formerly Family Service Association of America). For the location of the nearest branch or referral to other reputable, nonprofit agencies in your area, write: FSA, 11700 West Lake Park Drive, Milwaukee, Wisconsin 53224. Enclose a self-addressed, stamped envelope.

There are for-profit credit counseling agencies as well. Some charge fees ranging from 10 to 25 percent of your total debt. For-profits generally do not have the wide support of credit grantors, who reason that paying such high fees may force indebted consumers deeper into trouble.

PART TWO

Financial Security: A Matter of Age, Experience (and Lifelong Planning)

WHEN at nineteen years of age we assert with great authority what we plan to do with our lives, we are usually unaware of the life experiences that await us. But they are there. Financial planning must be done in pencil—and with a pencil that sports an oversized eraser.

Nevertheless, plan we must. For without doing so, none of the nineteen-year-old's dreams will be realized. Those life experiences that would, at times, interrupt, and, other times, enrich our lives would be dominated by financial pressures.

How the typical life experiences affect the financial factors in your life and what you can do to understand and prepare for them is the basis of this section.

Keep in mind that the planning is not all-inclusive, nor was it meant to be. Your individual situation may require planning that varies from our advice. As needed, consult with qualified financial planners, bankers, insurance agents, stockbrokers, realtors, lawyers, accountants, and other advisors. Pencils ready?

On Your Own ◆◆◆◆

THIS is the first summer vacation that won't end with the "back to school" blues. Instead, your thoughts are focused on starting out on your own. This is *the* time in your life to learn about managing money.

Rent and utilities will be your first and largest continuing expense. Set a ceiling on what you can spend—a very conservative level: *monthly rent that's no more than one week's gross pay or a week and a half's take-home pay.*

If using this rule you still can't find an affordable place, think about sharing with roommates, or, if necessary, stay home a little longer and save a little more.

Once you've found a place, you'll want to furnish it. Be creative. Shop secondhand.

Investigate tenants' property and liability insurance.

If you've moved to a new area, check on local doctors, dentists, etc. Find out if you have health coverage through work, or are still covered by your parents' policy. If neither, research health plans.

Open checking and savings accounts. A checking account makes paying bills convenient and easy.

Make savings part of your fixed monthly expenses. The day you cash your paycheck or deposit into your checking account make a deposit into your savings (or money market) account.

Your expenses will fluctuate with day-to-day living; some weeks you'll spend more on food, clothing, gifts, etc., than others. Don't expect to deal with these expenses effectively without budgeting. (See Table 1.)

Credit—how to get it, keep it, and not abuse it—is an aspect of finances to approach squarely.

The number-one rule for proper credit management is never overextend yourself. In addition, borrow only if:

TABLE 1 FOUR SAMPLE BUDGETS (Figures represent % of income)				
Budget Items	1	2	3	4
Housing and utilities	24	25	23	15
Food at home and away	11	10	15	15
Apparel—purchases and care	4	4	5	3
Personal care and grooming	2	2	2	2
Health care	1	2	4	5
Transportation	14	7	8	17
Leisure	10	5	5	4
Insurance	2	3	2	3
Savings and investment	3	5	3	1
Miscellaneous	7	5	3	14
Income taxes and pay deductions	22	32	30	21

1—Single, early 20s, income $20,000 a year.
2—Couple, late 30s, one works, income $40,000 a year.
3—Family, middle 40s, 1 child, both work, income $50,000 a year.
4—Couple, late 60s, both retired, income $30,000 a year.

◆ You are certain, within reason, that you will be able to repay the debt.
◆ You have thought through your purchase carefully. (Borrowing on impulse, or to lift your spirits, can backfire; you can get even more depressed when the bills come due.)
◆ The money is to be used for a purchase of enduring value. (Borrowing to finance a vacation, for example, is a bad idea, because your resolve to repay may evaporate as soon as the vacation ends.)

And never borrow money to invest in risky ventures.
Establishing credit is often tough for first-timers. Depart-

ment store credit cards are the easiest to obtain. By using one wisely, you may then become eligible for other types of credit.

Or you could borrow from a bank, a nominal sum of $500, for example, and ask a parent to cosign, if your being employed isn't sufficient. Then put the money into a savings or money market account and draw on it to make regular repayments on your bank loan. You lose a minor amount of interest, but it's a way of establishing credit if you can't get a credit card.

Mingled Singles ♦♦♦♦

MAKING the emotional commitment to live together may seem easier than working out the financial details involved.

Figuring out how expenses will be shared and drawing up a budget require careful planning, periodic review, and, if need be, revision. You should be confident that you are both living by the same fiscal rules.

Since most cohabiting couples have two incomes on which to draw, common arrangements include setting up a kitty for food and daily expenses and maintaining a joint checking account to pay for shared living expenses and purchases. In a typical case, each keeps a separate checking account and credit card for personal expenses—clothes, medical bills, presents, and the like. Cohabitants can't share health insurance policies, or file joint tax returns; and a divorced parent may lose child support when he or she moves in with a new partner.

Many couples eventually buy property together. Surprisingly, perhaps, single people buying a home together have proven to be among the safest mortgage risks. That serious a financial commitment presupposes an equally serious emotional one; nevertheless, smart couples make plans for disposing of the property in case they separate. Your real estate lawyer can draw up an agreement that protects each partner's interest.

While anticipating a breakup may not add to your romance, protecting what belongs to you is important. If you combine households, itemize who brought the microwave, who donated the television, and the like. To avoid messy arguments later, decide on ownership when subsequent purchases are made and make a mutually prepared list.

It may seem, too, that cohabitants need not bother with

wills and estate planning. Not true. In all fifty states, if a "spouse equivalent" dies, the survivor has no legal right to any property held in the deceased's name, even if it was acquired jointly. Some states permit an oral contract to suffice as proof of joint ownership; find out what laws apply in your state. In any event, if you want to share your estate, make a will.

As a cohabitant, you can't receive government benefits based on family relationships. That means no Social Security survivors, death, disability, or old-age benefits. Private employee benefits generally don't extend to unmarried couples, but you *can* name your partner as the beneficiary of your life insurance policy.

You Get Married ◆◆◆◆

YOUR friends and relatives aren't the only people who should be sent wedding announcements. You should also notify anyone involved with your finances that your status is changing.

First, take care of the routine business:

—Talk to your insurance agents and employment benefits specialists to make sure you are not paying for overlapping life, health, and other insurance coverage.

—Notify the Social Security Administration of your marriage so you'll be eligible for your spouse's benefits.

—Write or rewrite your will as necessary to include your new spouse.

—Add your spouse as beneficiary on your company pension and profit-sharing plans.

—A woman who changes her name at marriage should make the change on her driver's license, credit cards, employment records, and all other identification.

Establishing joint checking and savings or money market accounts can give you more borrowing and investment power. This is particularly important for a wife who will be a homemaker. If you both work, you should decide how much each of you will deposit in both accounts every payday. The amount put into your checking account should be enough to cover fixed monthly expenses, and allow for an accumulation of savings.

This is only the beginning.

To get your marriage off to a sound start, establish good communication and cooperative planning in all areas—especially financial.

Discuss your goals and priorities for tomorrow, next year,

and the years ahead. These can range from buying your own home to raising children to starting your own business. Whatever your goals are, identify them and aim to work together to attain them.

Investments. Before you actually make any, be sure to:

—Set aside funds for emergencies and make sure health, life, house, and car insurance needs are covered. For more on these subjects, see Part Four.

—Determine your temperament for risk. Does the idea of risking money for a potentially higher return make you lose sleep?

—Carve at least these rules of investing into your memory: (1) Become knowledgeable; (2) realize the risks of what you're getting into; (3) don't take advice or tips without investigating them yourself; and (4) diversify.

One way to start investing, and a way you can continue throughout your lifetime, is in mutual funds.

Mutual funds provide you with the advantages of choices to meet your objectives (see Table 2); professional management; diversified investment portfolios; the ability to invest in small amounts; the convenience of buying directly; handy record-keeping; the saving on brokerage commissions by their buying and selling securities in quantity; and liquidity (being able to convert your shares quickly into cash).

Information on mutual funds is available from the Investment Company Institute, 1600 M Street, N.W., Washington, D.C. 10036, and from the No-Load Mutual Fund Association, Inc., Room 2204, Penn Plaza, New York, New York 10001.

Joining an investment club is another good way you and your spouse can start investing, learn about the stock market—and meet new people. Most clubs have ten to twenty members who agree to invest a set amount—often as little as twenty-five dollars—each month. Members then meet regularly to exchange ideas, listen to guest speakers (often brokers looking for new clients), and to plan their investments.

For more information on how to start or join a club, contact the National Association of Investment Clubs, 1515 Eleven Mile Road, P.O. Box 220, Royal Oak, Michigan 48068.

You Have Children ◆◆◆◆

BEHIND that cuddly, lovable, cherished infant is an awesome responsibility and a staggering financial commitment.

Whether it's directly—through food, pediatricians, cub or Brownie scout uniforms, piano lessons, sneakers, schools, toys, and the like—or indirectly—through larger housing, more hot water for baths, larger phone bills, increased insurance coverage, child care, and more—you will be paying dearly.

Those costs are only part of the economic story. If a working mother has to leave work to rear a child, that means lost family income—not to mention the possibility of lost skills, if the woman is working in a rapidly changing career area. In many cases, mothers who had planned to take off a year or more to rear a child, or children, have returned to work months later because both husband and wife feel too pressured by the loss of the two salaries to which they have become accustomed. Nearly 70 percent of new mothers who take leave from work are back on the job within four months after giving birth. If the wife does go back to work and you pay someone to care for your child, you probably are entitled to a tax credit. Families with adjusted gross income of $28,000 or more get credit for 20 percent of their child care costs. The maximum tax credit for one child is $480; for two or more, it's $960.

That's why wives and husbands have to decide whether they should postpone having kids until they're economically better prepared. Or have fewer children. Or should the wife postpone her career until their last child is at least in kindergarten?

Before you sway under the weighty figures of child rearing, know that the costs start off manageable. Even though the experience of giving birth—hospital, routine delivery—may run around $2,500, most health/major medical insurance policies cover a large portion of the expense. But make certain you have the maternity benefits *before* the pregnancy. Once the wife is pregnant, it is too late to get or to increase maternity benefits on your health insurance. As soon as your baby is born, add him or her to your health/major medical insurance, reassess your life insurance (see page 125) and disability insurance needs, revamp your budget, and revise your will. The "Entertainment" category now includes a good baby-sitter.

And while the cost of baby clothes, special formulas, equipment, and nurses may seem burdensome now, expenses really climb in the teen years. For example, in moderate-cost areas, expenses for a child from birth to age one run around $4,700; but for ages sixteen and seventeen, around $6,700 per year.

Higher education makes up a major part of those expenses. Indeed, nothing can rock the financial stability boat more savagely and persistently than college costs for your children. That's why early planning and saving is essential.

Despite low inflation, college bills rose 7 percent in 1985 and 6 percent in 1986. The current average total cost for a year at a private college is $10,200. And some financial advisors project that future college expenses will increase even more rapidly than inflation and income.

What was already a heavy burden grew more onerous after the 1986 tax reform, which severely curtailed parents' ability to shift income to children and use the resulting tax savings for college.

Fortunately some tax-wise moves are still available.

For example, the effectiveness of custodial accounts, an income-shifting device, though curtailed, is still viable. Under tax reform anything over the first $1,000 income on gifts to children under fourteen will be taxed at the parents' top rate, which will be as high as 38.5 percent in 1987 and 33 percent beginning in 1988. The custodial account has one principal drawback: The child is entitled to do as he or she pleases with the money at age eighteen or twenty-one, depending on state law.

That $1,000, however, is better than nothing. Parents (or anybody else) may still give $10,000 annually per person to each child—free of gift tax. At 7 percent interest, $20,000 generates $1,400 of income, almost all tax-free.

AFTER AGE FOURTEEN TAX RULES CHANGE

When your child turns fourteen, all income on gifts from you or anyone else will be taxed at his or her generally much lower rate. Then parents can transfer larger sums of money to their children's custodial accounts. Parents and others can help by providing older children with some employment or odd jobs throughout the year. "You may want to encourage your child to work for a share of the educational costs," suggests Sidney Kess, a partner at KMG Main Hurdman, an accounting firm in New York City.

But keep in mind a tax-law change. Any child claimed as a dependent on a parent's tax return may not use the personal exemption.

INVESTMENT POSSIBILITIES

When parents give money to a child under fourteen, the general rule of thumb is to invest it in reasonably secure vehicles that pay little or no current income, but have good appreciation potential. Your first priority, of course, is to use up the annual $1,000 tax exemption on income from investments. For this purpose, investments paying currently taxable income up to that limit would also be desirable.

When your child turns fourteen, income becomes the name of the game because of the favorable tax rate. By then, safety and predictability become more important because you have less time to accumulate college funds.

What are today's sound investments for a child's college fund?

U.S. Savings Bonds. If owned by the child, you can defer tax payments on the interest until the Series EE bonds mature, which can be after your offspring turns fourteen and the lower tax rate kicks in. Or if your child's income is below $1,000, you could claim the interest annually (since there would be no tax due).

Municipal bonds. You may as well keep these in your name, since interest is tax exempt from federal tax—and if issued by your resident location, from state and local taxes, too. Most parents should avoid individual issues and choose municipal bond mutual funds or unit trusts instead. A bond fund that reinvests the interest and taxable capital gains is good because the manager can take advantage of interest rate trends.

Otherwise, consider a unit trust. It allows you to lock in a specific rate if you hold it to maturity. Unit trusts, sold through brokers, are available in many maturities.

Taxable bonds. Mutual funds are probably the best way for you to invest in corporate bonds. Be prepared to adjust your holdings as called for by rate trends and changing economic conditions. High-yield (junk bond) funds, for example, can be riskier but a good way to maximize current income if a recession is unlikely. Treasury securities funds are more suitable if the economy weakens.

Stocks and equity funds. Individual stocks, risky by virtue of their lack of diversification, are feasible if your investment record is solid. If individual stocks make you wary, diversification among growth and income mutual funds with good long-term records should provide good returns over the long haul. You also might consider mutual funds specializing in bonds and preferred stocks convertible into common stocks.

Single-premium deferred annuities (SPDAs) or life insurance. You can buy SPDAs with a lump sum of at least $5,000. Tax is paid only at withdrawal, based on the holder's bracket. New SPDAs currently pay about 8 percent, but the rate is guaranteed for a specific period of less than a year to five years. After that, rates depend on investment results, usually with a floor of 3–4 percent.

Single-premium life insurance may appeal to people willing to combine life coverage of their own with a college savings plan for a child.

WHEN COLLEGE LOOMS

What if your child already has been accepted at college and you need to raise cash quickly? One possibility is to take out a home equity loan. "Under the new tax law, interest would be deductible as long as the loan is secured by the residence," Kess points out.

Your First Home ◆◆◆◆

FINDING, funding, and following up: these are three crucial considerations when making your first home purchase.

1. Finding it. Neighborhood is a crucial factor for this investment. Investigate the economic stability of the community you intend to become a part of—departing businesses, reduced public transportation, building of cheaper houses, etc., may signal *decline*.

You may find a "steal" in a neighborhood that seems to be improving and end up a real winner, but be forewarned: Areas which appear to be on the upswing may not live up to their promise.

Homes can *depreciate* in value, too.

Before you buy a house, thoroughly inspect it—from flue to fuse box to foundation—or hire an expert to do the job. If a serious defect is discovered, try to negotiate a reduction in price. However, if the problem is too serious, you may decide not to buy the house.

If you're having a home built to your specifications, be sure you're ready for the experience. (You are *not* ready unless you're willing to spend many hours of supervision at the construction site.) Thoroughly research architects, builders, and contractors. Have everything put in writing: what it will cost, what materials will be used, when it will be completed, what warranties protect you, etc. Keep in mind that any variations from the architects' original plans will cost you dearly.

2. Funding it. Before you make any commitments to buy, investigate closing, mortgage, property tax, utility, and improvement costs.

Closing costs average several thousand dollars, and must be

paid in full at the time of closing. Don't forget, you'll need money to move in at this time, too.

Mortgages come in many forms. You should investigate as many lenders and plans as you possibly can. As you look at each of them, ask these questions:

—What's the most burdensome possible payment I would have to make? Could I afford that?

—How much interest will I have to pay? (Could I afford a plan that has higher but fewer payments, resulting in less overall interest?

—Does the contract have any "catches" that could harm me, such as penalties for prepayment, or clauses that allow the loan to be recalled?

Taxes—investigate how much they are before you buy and try to get an idea of how much they will increase from year to year by studying past records.

Find out what a good homeowners insurance policy will cost. (For more on homeowners insurance, see page 148.) Be sure you are covered in case a neighbor has an accident on your property, or in the event of a fire, flood, robbery, etc. Read the fine print of your policy.

Plan to have "home" reserves—$2,000 to $3,000 in savings—available for upkeep, emergencies, and improvements.

How Much Mortgage, Insurance, and Tax Costs Can You Carry?

To be comfortable financially with your home purchase, the costs of your mortgage principal and interest, homeowners insurance, and real-estate taxes, figured on a monthly basis, should not exceed 28 percent of your gross monthly income.

For example: Your gross monthly income is $3,000. Therefore, you could afford to pay up to $840 a month. Say you buy a home for $62,500, pay $12,500 down (20 percent of purchase price), and take out a $50,000 (80 percent) thirty-year, fixed-rate mortgage at a 13½ percent interest rate. Your monthly payment for mortgage principal and interest might be approximately $575. If your insurance was $20 and your taxes $200, your total monthly costs would be $795, or 26.5 percent of your $3,000 income. You could carry that.

But: If you bought a $100,000 home and took out an $80,000, thirty-year, fixed-rate mortgage at a 13½ percent interest rate, your monthly mortgage payment might be approximately $920, your insurance $30, and your taxes $320, for a total of $1,270— or about 42.3 percent of your $3,000 monthly income. You couldn't carry that.

3. Follow up. If you itemize deductions on your tax return, you can deduct property taxes, mortgage interest payments, interest on home-improvement loans, and even moving expenses (if because of a job you've relocated at least thirty-five miles more than the distance between your previous job location and your prior home).

Always keep your eye on mortgage rates. If the rates drop, you might be able to benefit from refinancing your mortgage.

If you get an increase in salary or cash supply, consider using this money to pay more of your mortgage principal, which can reduce your interest. See if your mortgage has any prepayment penalty clauses.

One last item: Review your property insurance periodically to see if it needs updating. As your house's value and its contents appreciate, you'll want to insure it for more. Review your liability coverage at the same time to see if it requires updating, too. (See page 154 for more on liability insurance.)

Career Gains ◆◆◆◆

CONGRATULATIONS. You've just received a big raise, landed a higher-paying job with another company, begun a money-making sideline, or turned the bottom line of your business balance sheet from red to black.

Now it's time for some personal financial moves of commensurate importance. Place these three tasks on your to-do list: Shield a portion of increased income from taxes; consider funneling some of your income into more aggressive investments; and take out more life insurance to protect your family's increased standard of living.

TAX SHELTERING

Consider opening one or more individual retirement accounts (IRAs) to shield up to $2,000 each year of your earnings and resulting returns (interest, dividends, etc.) from taxes—if you haven't already done so. You can contribute an additional $250 for a nonworking spouse. If both you and your spouse are working, each can contribute up to $2,000—together, $4,000. Individuals covered by employer plans and whose income exceeds $25,000 and married couples with income in excess of $40,000 may not be eligible for the full IRA deductions (but earnings on your contributions *will* compound tax-deferred).

And if you're self-employed, full-time or part-time, you can contribute up to 25 percent of this earned income into a Keogh plan (maximum contribution $30,000 yearly).

You're not taxed on these IRA and Keogh contributions and their earnings until you start withdrawing for retirement, when, presumably, you'll be taxed in a lower bracket.

You should take advantage of all tax-deferred compensation plans that may be available through your employment, such as a 401(k).

In addition, you can start investing in tax-favored investments yourself:

◆ Tax-deferred investments—such as annuities; universal, variable, and variable-universal life insurance; U.S. Savings Bonds; and exchanging (swapping instead of selling) real estate.

◆ Tax-advantaged securities—municipal bonds; dividend tax-free utility stocks; and tax-exempt money market, tax-exempt bond, single-state municipal, tax-managed, and tax-qualified mutual funds.

◆ Tax shelters—real estate, oil and gas, equipment leasing, and other limited partnerships. The 1986 tax reform legislation put a crimp into many of these, so be sure to consult your tax advisor before investing. Under the new law you're only able to deduct shelter losses up to the amount of your income from similar so-called passive investments (those in which you take no active role).

A NEW INVESTMENT STRATEGY

The increased earnings from your career advance can translate into more than greater disposable income, if you invest some of this money aggressively. Your goal: achieving maximum capital growth.

Two simple ways to increase the potential return (and risk level) of your investments is to buy shares in mutual funds with the objective of maximum capital gains, and join, or help form, an investment club accepting larger amounts from members and seeking greater returns.

In addition, you might join the American Association of Individual Investors, 612 North Michigan Avenue, Chicago, Illinois 60611, a not-for-profit corporation, whose offerings and those of local AAII chapters include publications, seminars, and home study materials to help members become more knowledgeable investors.

If you're planning to invest actively in individual securities or other mediums (stock options, stock indexes, financial futures, commodities, precious metals, real estate, limited partnerships, collectibles, etc.) you must "spend" time as well as money. Study *The Wall Street Journal*, business and financial sections of your daily newspapers, business and financial magazines, trade publications, market letters and research reports of stockbrokers, investment advisory publications and services, etc. You also may have to consult with professional advisors.

A more conservative route is to consider opening new IRAs or Keogh accounts and funding them with more aggressive investments. The difference in returns, over the long term, can be substantial. For example, $2,000 invested annually in an IRA or Keogh earning 8 percent a year would be worth $259,291 after thirty years, but a 12 percent return would be worth $620,730. Warning: Although you want to get the best return possible, don't jeopardize funds you're building for retirement.

LIFE INSURANCE

Your increased income probably will result in a more affluent life-style, and you'll have to take out more life insurance to protect your family accordingly (See page 125.)

You Get Divorced ◆ ◆ ◆ ◆

THE emotional impact of a divorce is often so strong that all practical matters pale in comparison. But when it comes to finances, it's vital that you be prepared to meet the complexities and challenges this situation provokes.

First, you should anticipate a heavy outlay for legal fees. While the price for an uncontested divorce may be as low as $150, a divorce that's battled out in the courtroom may run as high as $20,000.

Once the divorce is final, tax ramifications must be dealt with. The person paying alimony may deduct it; the person receiving payments must report them as taxable income.

Child support need not be reported and is not deductible. In many states, the transfer of property in "lump-sum settlements" is not considered a gift but a sale for which you are expected to pay capital gains tax. (That can be considerable, so know your state's tax laws before agreeing on a property settlement.)

Division of property often proves a stumbling block in divorce. If you and your spouse cannot come to terms, you may be able to ask the court for an "equitable distribution" settlement. This provides for a no-fault dissolution of the marriage and distribution of assets, and is based on contribution to the union, rather than culpability for the divorce. The idea is that any property accumulated during the marriage should be divided so that each partner can proceed with the next phase of life without financial ties.

Factors such as age and health of the couple, duration of the marriage, contribution of each to the career of the other, custody of the children, and loss of job potential are considered by the court in the division of assets. Be aware, however, that

❖ —————————————————————————— **65**

"equitable" doesn't mean "equal." What's "equitable" will often be decided solely by the judge's prejudices and predispositions.

In an increasing number of cases, equitable distribution is being favored over alimony in property settlements, with temporary alimony as a bridge to support a dependent spouse until she or he can complete an education or get a job. This is becoming more common than the traditional long-term alimony.

The prevalence of divorce has resulted in an upsurge of prenuptial agreements. An extension of prenuptial agreements is periodic inventory of assets and liabilities with the spouses agreeing to the values in writing.

The period of separation and divorce is most trying. The more you can separate the financial aspects from the emotional ones, the better off you'll be.

Going Back to Work ◆◆◆◆

MOST—though not all—of you who are returning to work are women. Whether you are returning because your children have left home, because your maternity leave has ended, or because you suddenly want to be more than a full-time home-maker, there is one certainty: When a wife also becomes a working woman/mother, the family and its finances are deeply affected.

On the plus side:

◆ There's another paycheck to help pay for everything from milk to the mortgage.
◆ If you pay someone to care for your children who are age fourteen or younger, you are entitled to a tax credit.

On the minus side:

◆ Your work skills may have atrophied and you may have lost your status in the working "pecking order," if you haven't worked for a while.
◆ You'll have to spend some of the salary on work-related items such as clothes, transportation, child care, lunches out, etc.
◆ You will have less time to comparison-shop and prepare meals, so you may have to spend more on lower-quality conve-nience foods.
◆ Your salary, when added to your husband's, may cause a jump in your tax bracket, which in turn reduces what you are actually contributing to the family income.
◆ You may encounter resistance in your family just when you need encouragement. Your husband and children may resent not being the center of your attention any longer. You may find them reluctant to take on chores you used to do by

yourself—and yet just as reluctant to lose the luxuries that your salary now makes possible.

For many women, to work or not to work is not the question: the family needs the added income and that's that. But even when the decision is hers to make, recent surveys show that women choose work over staying at home. And when your family solidly supports you, the "minuses" become minor next to the "pluses."

Children Off to College ◆◆◆◆

IF you started putting money away when your child was a youngster, and have continued to do so regularly over the years, it was one of the best "investments" you ever made. (The average person with a college education earns $142,000 to $329,000 more in a lifetime than a high school-educated counterpart.) If you don't have the money, though, there are a variety of options you and your child can take to fund an education.

Financial aid for both colleges and vocational schools is available from the federal government; state governments; college or vocational schools; community or private groups. And it comes in three basic forms:

—Grants. Based on financial need. Needn't be repaid.

—Scholarships. Based on talent, ability, or financial need. Needn't be repaid.

—Loans. Interest rates and starting dates for repayment vary, depending on the loan program.

For current information on federal programs, including loans, call the Student Information Center (301) 984-4070. For information on state assistance, call your state's department of education.

Your child should apply for state grants and scholarships first. Then tap private sources of grants and scholarships—though this money is harder to get. Start with the colleges themselves.

Also check into scholarships offered by labor unions, trade associations, and civic, fraternal, and national minority organizations. If you're employed by a corporation, find out if your company awards scholarships to children of employees. If your child scores well on the Scholastic Aptitude Tests (SATs), he or she might be eligible for one of the five thousand scholarships offered by the National Merit Scholarship Corporation.

Loans are the next resort. Seek funds from the federal government first, because it usually offers the best rates and terms. Then see if you and/or your child quality for: a low-interest loan from your child's college, local civic or religious groups, or a credit union; a deferred tuition plan, offered by a number of schools, that your child can help pay back after graduation; a bank or financial company loan—but only if all else fails, since their rates will be the stiffest.

Some cardinal rules for going after college financing:

1. Ask every school your child applies to for complete financial aid information.
2. Do not prejudge your eligibility for financial aid.
3. File all the forms requested, using the most accurate data you can provide. These forms are strictly confidential.
4. Make sure you meet all deadlines.
5. Keep good records of what you sent, where you sent it, and when.
6. Reapply for financial aid every year. Some aid is not automatically renewed each year.
7. Respond as quickly as possible to all requests made by the financial aid office.
8. Explore all avenues, comparison-shop loans, and don't get discouraged. There's always *some way* to get money for your child's education!
9. Consult your child's high school guidance counselor, and the financial aid administrator of the school your child selects. It's their business to know all about grants, scholarships, and loans.

Reversals ◆◆◆◆

MOST of life's difficult, challenging, or painful reversals (in health, career, family life, or investments) are unanticipated. That's why it's important to take precautionary steps to protect yourself, your family, and your assets from a future calamity.

If you depend on income from your job, the single most important step is to obtain disability insurance. Should you be hit by a long-term disability during your working years, you'll need this in addition to adequate health and life insurance coverage. (For more on disability insurance, see page 120.)

Not everyone can buy disability insurance, however. Among those who usually can't get it are individuals making less than $18,000 annually, and homemakers. Free-lancers of all kinds may find it difficult to find insurance. If they do, premiums may be higher than average.

Poor investments or loss of your job can lead to financial disability. Financial counselors recommend that you keep enough money in liquid savings and investments to tide you over for a minimum of three months. Six months is better. In the event of a financial disaster and short-term need, you can even borrow against your IRA or Keogh. The penalty for early withdrawal is 10 percent of the amount you withdraw and, of course, the money becomes subject to taxation, unless you could structure this as a "rollover." In a rollover, you have up to sixty days to transfer your IRA funds to another account before it's considered a withdrawal and, thus, subject to tax.

If a reversal threatens your previously sound credit rating, tighten your budget and hide your charge cards. If your situation is serious enough, you may want to consult a credit counselor. (See page 44.)

In the most extreme cases of financial overextension, bankruptcy may be the only answer. Though it provides you with a fresh start, and you can't be punished for choosing this option (for example, you can't lose your job), it stays on your credit record for up to ten years and, consequently, can hamper your financial health during that time.

In your "disaster planning" don't overlook protecting your house and assets from natural catastrophes.

You Remarry ◆◆◆◆

CONFLICTS of financial interest most commonly occur in a second marriage when former spouses and children are involved.

He may want a new car, but her child needs braces.

She may want a Caribbean vacation, but he needs the money to make an alimony payment.

The variations are endless and can be explosive threats unless financial obligations are understood and accepted from the outset.

Two emotional pitfalls that can lead to financial tension in a second marriage:

◆ Resentment of alimony payments. Unless you and your spouse want to enter a court and battle for renegotiation—for which you'll pay dearly both emotionally and financially—you simply must accept alimony as a fixed monthly expense. Make paying it as routine, unemotional, and automatic as paying the rent or telephone bill.

◆ Resentment of child-care costs. Children, from the cradle to college, are expensive. Whether they are yours or not, providing for them is part of the responsibility and reality of a second marriage.

If you do have children from a previous marriage, you may want to make special provisions for them in your will. One option is to set up a trust that enables a remarried person to bequeath income interest in property to a spouse without giving him or her actual control over the property. Instead, these trusts designate that the principal passes on to the children after the death of the heir. In this way you make certain that, after your death, your second spouse is financially taken care of, but that ultimately your estate will pass to your children from your first marriage.

Dealing with your own spouse's or your own "past life" in a new marriage can be difficult at times. The less you dwell on and resist the expenses stemming from a previous marriage, the better off you'll be.

If you find it hard to put the past in its place, consider turning to a self-help group, family counseling, a trusted friend, or a local chapter of the Stepfamily Association of America. This national not-for-profit organization provides educational and emotional support to stepfamilies. For information, send a self-addressed stamped envelope to: Stepfamily Association of America, 28 Allegheny Avenue, Towson, Maryland 21204.

Helping Elderly Parents ◆◆◆◆

NO help is more difficult to give—or to receive—than that offered by a grown child to an aging parent. Reversing roles with your parents, where you become the beneficent father or mother and your parent the dependent child, is so threatening to both sides that otherwise sensible people often make foolish decisions, or omit important ones, to avoid facing the consequences.

To a parent, accepting aid underscores the loss of his or her power to live alone, to handle financial affairs, make decisions, and maintain autonomy. To sons and daughters, the new responsibilities signal the end of a buffer between themselves and their mortality. Not only must they be responsible for themselves and their children, but also for the very people they themselves had looked to for care.

If the problems surrounding an incapacitated parent were only physical and emotional, they would be difficult enough. But in today's world, an invalid parent, whether physically or mentally handicapped, could easily need upward of $40,000 per year for nursing-home care. And none of the custodial care expenses is covered by Medicare—or almost any other form of insurance. Add the financial burden to the emotional one, and the cost to even the most well-meaning, well-heeled son or daughter becomes staggering, if not overwhelming.

For this reason, it makes sense to open discussions with elderly parents about their finances, even if the subject previously has been taboo. Because the time when a parent begins to fail is so fraught with anxiety, contends New York City attorney Peter J. Strauss, that is the worst time to make any important decision. Rather, he suggests that parents and children get together and make plans for the parents' possible decline long before the fact. Only in that way can parents "maintain their autonomy and dignity and make their own decisions" about their life-style if or when they become unable to handle their affairs, asserts Strauss.

A TRUST THAT ANTICIPATES NEEDS

The legal mechanisms that Strauss suggests to execute their wishes are *living or inter vivos trusts* and *durable powers of attorney.* Funded with as little as one hundred dollars, the living trust documents the parents' decisions on how assets are to be managed by the trustees. While the parents are well, the trust is inactive, says Strauss. But it is triggered into action when an event—such as a diagnosis of Alzheimer's disease (a neurological illness that results in an inevitable decline in mental powers) or an incapacitating stroke, or simply the parent's desire to reduce his or her responsibilities—makes it clear that the trustmaker can no longer function alone. At that point, the power of attorney that was signed at the trust's inception is used to transfer all of the parent's assets to the trust, to be used in the way set down originally.

The trust might spell out to the trustees (often the children, although sometimes a friend, relative, or attorney) where the parent will live, the level of health care he or she will get, how much money will be spent each year in his or her behalf, the number and size of yearly gifts that can be made to children and grandchildren, and whether the trust's principal can be invaded for specific reasons.

Although inter vivos trusts are not usually established for tax purposes, some of the planning that goes into them can provide a variety of financial benefits. For example, having the trust distribute annual gifts to each child and grandchild can minimize estate taxes at the death of the parents.

The trust can also shelter the principal of one spouse if the other must enter a nursing home. Medicare will pay no expenses for custodial care in a nursing home. Neither will Medicaid, until the patient has used up all but a nominal amount of his or her assets. If the patient is married, in many states Medicaid considers that all assets are joint, and that 50 percent of them belong to each spouse: Thus, if one spouse requires nursing-home care and the couple had $100,000 to begin with, Medicaid would require that close to $50,000 be spent for the disabled partner before it starts to kick in. The trust prevents Medicaid from imposing that kind of rule, since the trust can stipulate that income-producing real estate (which is exempt under Medicaid rules) be purchased by the trust for the benefit of the intact spouse.

Medicaid is routinely denied to anyone who has transferred assets of more than $2,000 to another within two years of application. Large transfers—more than $12,000—may extend the period of ineligibility for more than two years. In New York State, for instance, every additional $2,000 in transfers means another month of Medicaid ineligibility—unless the sick person can prove that medical expenses equal the transferred amount.

Under the new tax laws, many of the devices children once used to assist parents while protecting their own assets are no longer allowed. Thus, Crown loans (interest-free demand loans) and Clifford trusts (money placed in ten-year-and-one-day trusts for the benefit of another) no longer qualify as tax-sheltered vehicles.

But there are still ways to help parents and take a tax deduction, too. One way is to buy your parents' home and rent it back to them. This transaction frees your parents' equity in their home, giving them a sum of money to invest or live on, while it provides you with all the tax deductions of rental-property ownership—tax deductions for interest, realty taxes, and depreciation—as well as reducing the income you get from the property by the maintenance costs.

But Strauss argues that this strategy would backfire if one parent entered a nursing home, since a home is an exempt asset when someone applies for Medicaid coverage, while cash is not.

MORTGAGES THAT PAY PARENTS

For that reason, Peter Strauss suggests reverse annuity mortgages (RAMs) as the solution for the elderly who are house-rich but cash-poor. RAMs work this way: Assume your parents own their own home free and clear, or have only a very small mortgage outstanding, and that the property is currently worth $150,000. They'll realize that (appreciated) value only if they sell. But instead of selling, they can borrow against the house, using it as collateral. Instead of giving them a lump sum, the bank will lend them up to 80 percent of the value of the house over, say, a ten-year period, in monthly install-ments, so that they have a nontaxable income stream coming in each month.

At the end of the ten-year period, their house has a mort-gage of $120,000 against it. But during that time, the value of the property will probably have appreciated as well—perhaps to $200,000 or more. At this point, your parents can sell and pay off the mortgage, or refinance the house and apply for another RAM.

SWITCHING FINANCIAL OBLIGATIONS

What if parents' assets are insufficient to maintain them com-fortably, and you are being squeezed by college costs for your own youngsters? By unofficially swapping burdens, you both come out ahead.

For example, assume you are paying $14,000 annually for your youngster's college tuition and room and board. Meanwhile, your parents receive $4,500 per year tax-free from a municipal bond fund in which they have $75,000 invested. Social Security pays them $6,000 per year, too. Although their actual income is $10,500, none of it is taxable. They put $5,000 in the bank each year, *which they don't touch.* Thus, for purposes of support, the IRS assumes they spend only $5,500 to maintain themselves, says Eli Warach, chief consulting editor, Prentice-Hall Information Services. If you put up $5,501 or more to support them each year, you can take them as your dependents, since they meet both of these tests:

1. They have taxable income of less than $1,080 in 1986; $1,900 in 1987; $1,950 in 1988; and $2,000 in 1989.
2. You contribute more than half toward their support.

During your youngster's college years, he or she can borrow $5,000 (or more) each year toward tuition, reducing the burden on you. On graduation your parents give their grandchild a present of the money they've put aside. They each can give the graduate $10,000 per year, which he or she can use to pay off the loans. Of course, their gift is not conditional on your support or vice versa.

Your parents' nest egg remains intact, and they have at least as much income—and perhaps more, if you share the tax savings with them—as they would otherwise have enjoyed.

Careful study of the new tax laws will almost certainly lead to further ways for you to provide support while minimizing the tax bite. But even without the new laws, some of the existing statues offer sensible ways to help.

One way to keep an eye on your aging parents while maintaining their independence is to have them live with you in their own quarters. If you can create an apartment for them within your own house and have them rent the apartment, part of your own home can be considered rental property. That enables you to depreciate a portion of the home as well as write off part of the taxes and maintenance against the rental income. At the same time, you can still contribute more than half of their support, and list them as dependents on your tax returns.

OTHER SAVVY WAYS TO HELP

Finally, there is a way to divvy up the responsibility of caring for your elderly parents among yourself and your siblings, while allowing a different sibling each year to enjoy the tax benefit. Assume that you and your brothers and sisters each contribute a portion of the sum toward your parents' maintenance. In total, you all supply more than 50 percent of their support, while each of you contributes at least 10 percent each year. To enjoy the tax benefit, all but one of you sign Form 2120, agreeing not to claim your parents on your returns. That enables the selected sibling to take the deduction for that particular year.

If all of this seems calculating, consider it another way: By providing for your parents, you are ensuring their standard of living. And by taking advantage of tax benefits, you may be able to offer them even more.

Your Children Become Independent ◆◆◆

YOUR children leave home, get married, and have children of their own—that's the storybook scenario. The reality is that your children may do none of, or only some of the above, and not necessarily in that order.

But if and when your last child leaves the nest, a number of changes occur in the character of your finances.

Your cash supply may increase. In part, this may be due to a drop in some expenses, such as health insurance premiums. But, because you can declare fewer dependents, you may have to pay more in taxes.

With your children gone, you'll need smaller cash reserves, and a homemaker-spouse may go back to work, increasing the family income. These added funds might be invested, perhaps more aggressively, since your expenses and obligations are less burdensome now.

It's time to think about your home—as an investment. Perhaps, with your children gone, it seems too large for you. Consider selling. If you bought a smaller home, or rented, the funds left over could be invested.

When your children marry, you may want to revise your estate plan and your will—especially if the newlyweds begin having children of their own. Many grandparents do make provisions for their grandchildren in their will. They don't necessarily include them as direct beneficiaries, but beneficiaries in the event that something happens to their parents. (For more on estate planning, see page 191.)

Into Your Retirement ....

THESE two rules of retirement point out why planning for yourself, in advance, is so important:

1. You can't expect to live on Social Security checks.

It's best to think of Social Security as it was intended—as supplemental income for retirement, not the financial foundation of it. For example, if over your career you earned enough each year to pay the maximum contribution and retired this year at age sixty-five, your estimated monthly Social Security check would be $739—considerably less than you have been accustomed to living on.

Also, the IRS started taxing some Social Security benefits for the first time in 1984. Now that the immunity has been breached, these taxes may well be increased in the future.

2. You can't count on your pension plan—for a number of reasons:

◆ Most pension payments don't amount to much; the average monthly pension check is estimated to be about $479.
◆ Company pension plans rarely keep up with the rise in the cost of living.
◆ Many pension plans are inadequately funded to provide promised future benefits. That means you might not be paid.
◆ If your company goes bankrupt, you could lose your pension.

(For more on pensions, see page 181.)

The key to good retirement planning is to structure your investments so you have a predictable stream of income to meet your needs. How much will you need? Here is a rough way of figuring:

❖

◆ Determine how much it would cost today to retire to the life-style you seek. Prepare an item-by-item expense checklist.

◆ Add up the number of years remaining until your retirement.

◆ Approximate what you think the annual rate of inflation will be over that period.

◆ Multiply the yearly number of dollars necessary for retirement by the inflation rate. For example, say it takes $100,000 principal for you to retire today, with interest or dividends from this sum added to your pension and Social Security income. Say the expected inflation rate is 6 percent. Multiply $100,000 by 1.06 on your calculator. Then take that new amount ($106,000) and multiply it by 1.06 again, and again for each year remaining until you retire. If you wanted that $100,000 ready in ten years, you would need to save $179,084 to get the present-day buying power of $100,000.

Another approach is to use Table 2, which shows how inflation shrinks your dollars. For example, say inflation averages 8 percent annually for the next fifteen years to when you retire and you have a $100,000 nest egg now. At that time, the purchasing power of your $100,000 nest egg would have been reduced to only $32,000 (32 cents on the dollar!).

How do you go about attaining your retirement goals?

First, you should take advantage of tax-favored investment means, such as IRAs; deferred employment-income plans, for example, 401(k)s; and, if you are self-employed, Keoghs.

Then, over the years, through these means and others, invest for capital growth, to exceed the effects of inflation and provide the principal that you can start converting to higher-income-paying investments as you near retirement.

As you survey your retirement assets, you should ask yourself some pointed questions. For example, regarding your home: Would a sale be prudent? Benefits include a surge in disposable funds and, if you are age fifty-five or older, and have lived

TABLE 2 HOW INFLATION SHRINKS YOUR DOLLAR							
What $1 is worth after these annual rates of inflation							
(Figures rounded to the nearest cent)							
Years	4%	5%	6%	7%	8%	9%	10%
1	96¢	95¢	94¢	94¢	93¢	92¢	91¢
2	93¢	91¢	89¢	87¢	86¢	84¢	83¢
3	89¢	86¢	84¢	82¢	79¢	77¢	75¢
4	86¢	82¢	79¢	76¢	74¢	71¢	68¢
5	82¢	78¢	75¢	71¢	68¢	65¢	62¢
6	79¢	75¢	71¢	67¢	63¢	60¢	56¢
7	76¢	71¢	67¢	62¢	58¢	55¢	51¢
8	73¢	68¢	63¢	58¢	54¢	50¢	47¢
9	70¢	65¢	59¢	54¢	50¢	46¢	42¢
10	68¢	61¢	56¢	51¢	46¢	42¢	39¢
15	56¢	48¢	42¢	36¢	32¢	28¢	24¢
20	46¢	38¢	31¢	26¢	22¢	18¢	15¢

% = annual inflation rate

in the house for three of the past five years, you may be eligible for tax benefits on up to $125,000 of the capital gain.

Can you cash in your life insurance policy or policies or draw on them for additional retirement income? This may be a wise move for you if your family no longer relies on you for financial support.

You'll want to be certain that you have adequate health insurance; realistically, this coverage becomes increasingly important as you age.

Thanks to legislation passed in 1986—Consolidated Omnibus Budget Reconciliation Act (COBRA)—retirees of companies with twenty or more employees have the right to extend their group health benefits for up to eighteen months. The cost, which the retiree must bear in full, is capped at no more than 2 percent above regular group rates. According to the law, the coverage must be identical to that you received as an employee.

Once the eighteen months expire, you can convert your group insurance coverage to an individual plan, if necessary—assuming your employer offers this option. Expect the cost of your health insurance to shoot up and the extent of coverage to narrow when you convert.

Medicare kicks in at age sixty-five, but it doesn't pay all the bills, so make sure your private policy picks up the tabs for most of what Medicare misses. (These policies are called "Medigap" policies.) For more information, contact the Health Insurance Association of America, 1025 Connecticut Avenue, 12th Floor, Washington, D.C. 20036.

Senior-citizen health and life insurance policies are available from various private companies and associations (such as the American Association of Retired Persons, 1909 K Street, N.W., Washington, D.C. 20049).

More and more retirees view the end of their primary career as a good opportunity to start up their own business—the one they've long dreamed of—or to go to work part-time in a new field that intrigues them. You can earn up to $6,000 a year if you're under sixty-five, and up to $8,160 a year from sixty-five to seventy and still draw full Social Security benefits. Once you turn seventy, you can earn any amount without losing benefits. (Keep in mind that if you earn over $25,000 as an individual, or over $32,000 as a couple, up to one half of your Social Security benefits can be subject to federal income tax.)

Death in the Family ◆◆◆◆

ONE of the most considerate gifts you can leave your family is a clear plan for handling your affairs after your death.

A will is a must. Without one, you have absolutely no control over how your property will be distributed. Your assets may become the target of taxes. Most important, you place your family in a tense, uncertain, and potentially divisive situation.

To provide and protect is the purpose of your will, so be sure it allows for clear, easy distribution of assets and liquidity; guarantees assets will be properly managed; assures reasonable continuation of your family's life-style; and minimizes or eliminates the burden of taxes.

If you are married, both you and your spouse should have wills.

You should own a family cemetery plot if you request burial in your will. Make sure you see the cemetery and the plot before you buy. Be careful about the contract's stipulations as to installment payments.

Another must: prearranged funeral services for burial or cremation. They will not only spare your bereaved family the effort and complication of making arrangements, they will shield them from making hasty and costly decisions. The average cost range of a funeral is a shocking $3,600 to $4,600.

A memorial society can make preplanning easy. These societies provide services, burial, cremation, and plots, with details on how much they cost. For more information, send a self-addressed envelope to the Continental Association of Funeral and Memorial Societies, 2001 S Street, N.W., Suite 530, Washington, D.C. 20009. In Canada, write to the Memorial Society Association of Canada, Box 96, Station A, Weston, Ontario M9N 3M6.

❖

If you decide to pay for funeral arrangements in advance, be sure that the money is placed in a special savings account so you, *not* the funeral director, collect the interest.

And before buying a funeral package or cemetery plot, find out what arrangements can be made if you move. Many cemeteries belong to a nationwide lot exchange program that allows individuals to trade plots in different areas.

When there's a death in the family, among many things you, as the surviving spouse or relative, must take care of:

◆ Obtain certified copies of the death certificate.
◆ Get the original copy of the will.
◆ Notify the deceased's lawyer, insurance agents, and accountant.
◆ Contact your local Social Security office to inform it of the death and to determine your eligibility for death or survivor benefits.
◆ Search for stocks, bonds, savings, certificates, passbooks, ownership deeds, and the like so you can create an inventory for estate purposes.
◆ Inform banks, brokerage houses, and other firms where the deceased had accounts, debts, loans, etc.
◆ Notify the deceased's employer and business associates and find out about death or any other benefits.
◆ If applicable, inform the Veterans Administration or other organizations regarding death benefits.
◆ File an income tax return on the deceased's behalf, if he or she received taxable income in the year of death.

Beware: As a survivor, this is a particularly emotional, difficult, and susceptible period in your life. Don't make any investments or loans; don't buy or sell any securities, annuities, or property; and don't convert any insurance policies *during this time.* Wait until you are in a more objective frame of mind and until you've had time to do research or consult with advisors.

PART THREE

Tools for Building Your Financial Security

QUESTION: Do you really need a $200 food processor to slice a lowly carrot? The question may sound absurd in the context of this book on financial security, but it's intended as an analogy:

Do you need a $200 food processor to slice a carrot, and, similarly, do you need the most sophisticated—and expensive—instruments available to achieve financial security?

The answer—we think most would agree—is no.

The surest route to financial security bypasses the razzmatazz of the latest financial products in favor of fundamentals.

That's what you'll find in this section: information on the basic tools of financial security. These tools remain the same at just about every stage of your life. What changes is how you apply them; and we address that issue here as well.

Putting Your Money to Work

◆ ◆ ◆ ◆

WITH today's constant barrage of new investment possibilities, it's easy to lose sight of one simple fact of financial life. There are basically two types of investments: those that produce income, and those that do not.

Income-producing investments include your bank and money market accounts, certificates of deposit, bonds, and most stocks and mutual funds.

Non-income-producers are your home and recreational property, cash-value life insurance, jewelry, and collectibles. While these do not bring in income, they are, after all, investments, and should at least be growing in value for you. (Also included in this category are those stocks and mutual funds that are not currently paying a dividend or very little, but which you are holding for their growth potential.)

How you should allocate your assets between these broad investment categories depends on your stage of life. If your salary is adequate to cover your expenses, you may want to concentrate assets in investments that will provide long-term capital growth and appreciation, rather than immediate income. When that changes, so, too, should your investing strategy.

Take the case of a young two-earner married couple. In all likelihood, they can anticipate a steadily growing income. This is a stage in their lives when they should look to investments that will build up capital for their future needs. The picture may change dramatically, however, when the couple's first child starts filling out college applications. At that point, they may need to shift some of their assets into income-generating investments, rather than try to defray years of staggering tuition bills entirely out of their salaries.

Once the children have gone out on their own, the couple's

financial outlook will take another significant turn. Not only will they no longer have to pay tuition bills, but their day-to-day living expenses should drop remarkably. As their nest empties, their nest egg will begin to fill up again.

Chances are, the couple will now have greater discretionary income than they have ever known. From this point, until they decide to retire, they will again want to invest for capital appreciation, in order to lay a foundation for their retirement years.

When they do retire, they will probably find that their pensions and Social Security checks don't add up to enough income to support the life-style they have come to expect. That means it's time to shift at least some of their assets back from growth investments to income-producing vehicles.

Using the Worksheet

So much for our fictitious couple. What about you? The worksheet on page 92 is designed to give you a quick roundup of your assets and the income you receive from them.

The first column, "Net Sale Value," should show an asset's worth after you have subtracted the costs associated with selling it. With stocks, for example, you will pay brokerage fees; with your home, legal expenses and real estate broker commissions. Even assets such as collectibles may incur selling costs, among them being auction or consignment fees. (You probably also should consider the effects of capital gains taxes.)

The second column, "Annual Income," is basically self-explanatory, but may require some rummaging through your financial records to come up with the numbers.

To determine just how hard your income-producing assets are working for you, use the third column, "% Yield." (To arrive at an investment's yield, divide the annual income it generates by its value. For example, if you have a $5,000 certificate of deposit that pays you $400 a year in interest, its yield is $400 ÷ $5,000 = 8 percent.) Even if you don't anticipate a need for a major shift in your assets, filling in this column

TABLE 3	ASSET EVALUATION WORKSHEET			
INCOME-PRODUCING ASSETS	**Net Sale Value**	**Annual Income**	**% Yield**	**Annual Cost of Ownership**
Checking Accounts	$	$		$
Savings Accounts				
Credit Union Accounts				
Money Market Accounts				
Certificates of Deposit				
Treasury Bills				
Treasury Notes				
Bonds				
Stocks				
Mutual Funds				
Rental Property				
Business Interests				
Other				
TOTAL				
NON-INCOME-PRODUCING ASSETS				
Personal Residence	$	$		$
Recreational Property				
Cash-Value Life Insurance				
Non-Income-Producing Stocks and Mutual Funds				
Home Furnishings				
Automobiles				
Jewelry				
Antiques				
Coin or Stamp Collection				
Fine Art				
Other				
TOTAL				

can help you spot a poorly performing investment that you may want to weed out of your portfolio.

The fourth column of the worksheet allows you to figure in the annual costs of owning each asset. In the case of income-producing assets, you will probably leave this column largely blank—unless you want to take into account their income tax ramifications (such as taxes on interest and dividends), which can considerably complicate this exercise.

Non-income-producers, however, have other costs attached to them that should be listed. These might include mortgage interest, real-estate taxes and upkeep expenses on your home, and premiums on your insurance.

(If you really enjoy playing with numbers, you may want to construct a more complex worksheet tailored to your own portfolio. Some investors may also find it revealing to compute after-tax yields on income-producing investments.)

When you have completed the worksheet, you should have a fairly clear picture of what your assets are up to. Should you make any changes? That, of course, depends on your personal circumstances, both current and foreseeable.

One thing always to keep in mind, though, is that no investment is forever. Do not feel married to an asset just because you have owned it for a while. Try as much as possible to examine each one objectively.

If a stock is no longer performing up to your expectations, consider unloading it in favor of a brighter prospect. And even if it's not here yet, the day will come when you'll need to take a hard look at what is probably your major asset: your home. Here, emotional attachments may be especially strong. But don't hesitate to ask yourself whether your home is too large for your needs or too costly to maintain. Does selling it and buying a smaller home make sense? Or selling your home, moving into a rental property, and investing the profit elsewhere?

By sitting down with a worksheet like this one for just a few minutes every year, you should be able to keep your financial picture in crisp focus. More important, you'll be ready to react quickly and profitably as your life progresses and your financial needs change.

SAVING AND INVESTING: HABITS THAT YIELD BIG DIVIDENDS

When saving becomes as routine to you as brushing your teeth, you're well on your way toward financial security. That's because the secret to building wealth through a conservative savings plan lies not so much in the amount you save (although that certainly makes a difference) as in the *regularity* with which you save. Small amounts, consistently invested, grow exponentially, thanks to the compounding income available on money market accounts, U.S. Savings Bonds purchased on a payroll savings plan, expandable certificates of deposit available at some savings institutions, and shares of income or income and growth mutual funds.

Though $100 may seem an insignificant sum to set aside each month, the opposite is true if you have time on your side, notes Inga H. Hanna, a Portland, Maine, certified financial planner. Consider this example: $100 invested each month at 7 percent and compounded monthly over fifteen years will grow to $31,696. That's $3,207 more than you'd accumulate if you made a one-time investment of $10,000 and left it to grow for fifteen years at the same compounded interest rate.

Managing Your Savings

Putting away money regularly is important, but so is deciding *where* to put it.

Saving isn't a matter of chucking pennies into a piggy bank. It's an active portfolio decision to place capital where it preserves value, ensures liquidity, and earns high returns. Almost

TABLE 4 THE BIG PAYOFF IN STEADY SAVINGS		
Interest Compounded Monthly	Column 1 $10,000 Invested Today	Column 2 $100 a Month Invested Every Month
After 10 years 7% 8% 9% 10%	20,097 22,196 24,514 27,070	17,308 18,295 19,351 20,484
After 15 years 7% 8% 9% 10%	28,489 33,069 38,380 44,539	31,696 34,604 37,841 41,447
After 20 years 7% 8% 9% 10%	40,387 49,268 60,092 73,281	52,093 58,902 66,789 75,937
After 25 years 7% 8% 9% 10%	57,254 73,402 94,084 120,569	81,007 95,103 112,112 132,683

Time Required for Amount in Column 2
to Be Greater Than Column 1

Rate	Time
7%	12 yrs., 7 mos.
8%	13 yrs., 10 mos.
9%	15 yrs., 6 mos.
10%	18 yrs., 0 mos.

Chart: Carteret Savings and Loan Association, Morristown, N.J.

by definition, smart savers are smart investors. They recognize the importance of savings, and they know that savings must be *managed* as astutely as any portfolio element. In managing savings, investors learn and follow techniques applicable to other portfolio decisions and maintain skills they need to make other elements of their portfolio profitable.

What we normally think of as "savings" is really a particular type of investment—namely, constant-dollar investments subject to minimal market risk. That's why savings are often called the stability element of the portfolio and considered as important as the capital growth and aggressive gains components of the portfolio.

The conventional passbook account with a bank or savings and loan or a share account with a credit union meet this need, but so do certificates of deposit and other depository accounts, money market accounts and mutual funds, near-term bonds, and short-term bond mutual funds. These types of investments offer several of the same advantages. They fluctuate minimally in price, if at all. They are liquid, provided you keep maturities short. They offer predictable yields. They are easily understood investments accessible to all investors, and they can be held without fees, although commissions apply to purchase and sale of bonds and some bond funds have sales charges (loads).

Their liquidity, predictability, simplicity, accessibility, and low cost make these investments ideal for the savings element of the portfolio. Nevertheless, they have important differences that affect the way you manage the savings component.

For one thing, each of these vehicles requires different minimums for initial investment. Passbook accounts and some money market accounts and mutual funds have no minimum for initial or subsequent investments, making them the preferred choice for first-time savers. Most money-market mutual funds and most bond funds require $1,000 to $2,500 initial minimums with subsequent investments of $100 to $500, although minimums are less for some funds. Direct purchase of near-term corporate, government, and municipal obligations is generally for the best-capitalized saver-investor, since these investments require at least a $10,000 commitment to be purchased efficiently.

Even though certificates of deposit are available from $500 upward, they present two problems as savings vehicles: You pay an interest penalty if you close a CD prior to maturity, and you can't add deposits to a CD until it matures. Therefore, saver-investors must restrict maturities on CDs to six months or so to ensure liquidity and ability to add to savings.

As you'd expect, the lower the initial investment, the lower the return on a savings vehicle. Lower return is the price you pay for higher availability. Passbook accounts still yield about 5½ percent compounded monthly, and most share accounts with credit unions offer 5 to 6 percent. Returns on money market mutual funds have varied from 5 to almost 20 percent since they first appeared, whereas short-term bond funds and bonds with near-term maturities have yielded 7–10 percent during this decade, which has been the normal range for short-term CDs as well.

Many advisors counsel investors to hold between 10 and 25 percent of their total portfolio value in savings, depending upon the investor's age and life circumstances. Others advise the equivalent of three to six months' net salary in constant-dollar investments, regardless of portfolio value.

To acquire adequate cash in savings-type investments, the best strategy is the "self-tithe"—setting aside 10 percent of net income every payday before you can spend it. The easiest way to implement the self-tithe is to participate in automatic deposit programs offered by depository institutions, money market funds, and short-term bond funds. These intermediaries will withdraw a specified amount from your checking account, usually on the first and/or fifteenth of the month.

Diversification is no advantage for the savings component of the portfolio, for constant-dollar investments are highly safe, but maximum safety is available in United States government obligations and government securites mutual funds. The key to effective management of the stability element of the portfolio is consolidating constant-dollar investments in one place. If you need to draw on your savings, having them in one vehicle makes them easy to get to. Also, having constant-dollar investments in one place makes it easier to move them to higher-paying investments.

Moving the savings component from one investment to another is an important part of managing the stability element of the portfolio. Many investments offer capital stability, but those with higher minimum investments sometimes pay greater returns. As you build up the stability element of your portfolio, you'll want to move your holdings into higher-yielding vehicles.

Savings from the ground up. Let's look at how you, as a beginning investor, might manage your savings over many years.

You begin by setting aside 10 percent of net salary each month, perhaps in a savings account or money market fund. When the savings account is large enough, you will move into a money market fund generally paying several percent more interest and generally requiring $1,000 as a minimum investment. As sums in the money fund increase, say to $5,000, you might move into a short-term bond fund or certificate of deposit, both of which offer a shade more interest than money market funds. Once the savings reach the $10,000 level, you will likely move into Treasury bills, larger-denomination CDs, short-term bonds, or mutual funds specializing in government securities or short-term corporate bonds.

However, you may be beyond this evolutionary development of a savings portfolio. Perhaps you want to take gains from well-chosen stocks or other investments and realign your portfolio to preserve your advances.

If you're holding $5,000 to $10,000, your best receptacle is the conventional money market fund. If you're after maximum security, consider a fund that invests exclusively in U.S. Treasury securities; and if you're in the higher tax brackets, select a tax-exempt money fund that purchases short-term municipal obligations. On an after-tax basis, these funds may provide higher returns while maintaining safety and liquidity.

With savings in the $5,000 to $10,000 range, you might also consider purchase of short-term bond funds—corporate bond funds if you're in modest tax brackets and municipal funds if you're not. These funds generally offer higher returns than money funds do, but their net asset values will fluctuate slightly with conditions. On the positive side, bond funds may provide capital appreciation in addition to regular interest. On the negative side, these funds may bring slight capital losses if interest rates rise. Therefore, both funds aren't the rock-solid constant-dollar investments that money funds are, even though their prices will fluctuate only minimally.

Investors with $10,000 or more to devote to the stability element of the portfolio might wish to invest in corporate, government, or municipal bonds with near-term maturities, but they must be wary of commissions, time-consuming paperwork, and slight delays in converting investments to cash.

To ease these constraints, go directly to the source. You can buy Treasury bills and short-term government bonds directly from the Federal Reserve Bank or branch nearest you, in person or by mail, without commissions. Maturities range from 90 days to one year in the case of T-bills ($10,000 minimum for investment), and commission-free Treasury notes are auctioned in two- and five-year maturities ($5,000 minimum investment). Interest on these instruments is exempt from state and local taxation, which adds to yield.

In the corporate market, you can buy blue-chip bonds without commissions when they're originally issued by a sponsoring brokerage, and the same is true for newly issued municipal obligations. Watch *The Wall Street Journal* or your local financial pages for announcements.

One word about municipal bonds and notes as savings instruments: resale. If you need to sell your municipal bonds, you get a better price if you're holding at least a $25,000 lot. If you aren't at that level in the savings component of your portfolio, better keep your municipal investments restricted to tax-exempt money funds or short-term municipal bond funds.

Whatever you do, reinvest interest from your savings instruments. This is no problem for savings accounts, CDs, and funds, since your distributions will be reinvested unless you specify otherwise. But if you're holding savings in directly owned short-term bonds, arrange to have the interest reinvested immediately in a money fund. Make the reinvestment rule, and keep it.

In short, the rules for managing the savings component of the portfolio are simple. Get your constant-dollar investments together. When they reach a critical investment mass, move them to the next-higher-paying vehicle, and then to the next, and so on. Your gains compound as your savings grow.

A Winning Investment System

If you're looking for an easy investment system you can follow all your life—one that works regardless of stock market conditions and one that frees you from the tedium of watching or timing the market, "dollar-cost averaging" is for you.

Use dollar-cost averaging when you invest in stocks or mutual funds. The system generally works better with equity mutual funds than individual stocks because their diversified holdings best reflect the overall stock market.

Here's what to do: Decide how much money you can comfortably invest at regular intervals. Select a day—the first of the month, for example—and a period of time—say, every month or two or so—then make your investments religiously according to that schedule. Never vary your schedule or neglect to invest, regardless of market fluctuations.

Continue your investment system over several years—*at minimum, five.* (Dollar-cost averaging is *not* for short-term investors or anyone looking for quick and spectacular gains.)

The long-term effect of this system is to *average out your costs,* because you end up buying fewer shares at higher prices; more shares at lower prices—with equal amounts of money (see Table 5). And the overall upward trend of the United States economy and the stock market means that stock prices should be much higher, on average, five or ten or fifteen years from now.

TABLE 5			
Date	Investment	Price Per Share	Shares Bought
Jan. 1	$100	$50	2
Feb. 1	100	40	2½
Mar. 1	100	40	2½
Apr. 1	100	25	4
May 1	100	30	3⅓
June 1	100	50	2
July 1	100	75	1⅓
	$700		17⅔

Note: Price swings have been exaggerated and commissions eliminated to dramatize dollar-cost averaging effects.

In this hypothetical example, the average price of your shares is $44.28 per share. But with your $700 total investment you have purchased 17⅔ shares, so each share has cost you just $39.63. Though you show a paper loss on April 1, you have earned a tidy profit by July 1.

Like other investment systems that tell you when—not what—to buy, dollar-cost averaging is fallible. You can lose with this system if your judgment is poor and the stocks or mutual funds you choose never realize their growth potential, or if you're forced to sell when the accumulated market value of your shares is less than your actual cost. So never commit funds to dollar-cost averaging that you may need for other purposes.

YOUR ANNUAL PORTFOLIO CHECKUP

You may undergo a medical checkup once a year and a dental checkup every six months or so. But have you ever considered a periodic portfolio checkup?

If not, you should. Properly done, it can be as important to your financial health as medical and dental checkups are to your physical health.

A periodic analysis of your stock and bond portfolio, which you can conduct yourself, is a great help in understanding your financial past, present, and future. It lets you relate the changes in your holdings to the changes in securities markets in general. Also it serves as the basis for the critical buy, hold, and sell decisions that you must make to keep your portfolio up-to-date.

"A portfolio, like a garden, has to be pruned regularly to keep it really strong," says William O. H. Freund, Jr., a senior vice presient of Prescott, Ball and Turben, Cleveland, Ohio, a large brokerage and investment banking firm. "You have to assess your portfolio against certain criteria—such as the quality of the balance sheet, the earnings trend, and the payout ratio—that you also would use when seeking new purchases."

"Weeding a portfolio is important, both from the point of view of taking a profit when it has been realized and cutting a loss when expectations have not been met," adds Robert B. Nelson, a partner of the Cleveland law firm of Jones, Day, Reavis and Pogue. "You're not buying last year's results, you're buying the current period of performance."

Although portfolio examinations are usually done on an annual basis—typically in December, when tax and other financial records are being gathered—some experts suggest that the checkup can be more useful if conducted quarterly, or even monthly. Their reasoning: Trends in the financial markets that previously took a long time to unfold now occur much more rapidly, with new market phases developing faster than ever before. Whatever frequency you select, the checkup must be conducted regularly and with the same points of reference each time.

"You have to decide the investment profile you're trying to achieve, then translate it into investment positions that actually make sense," notes Barry Sahgal, managing director for research at Ladenburg, Thalmann Company, a New York City securities concern. "It's a minefield out there. What kind of risk-reward ratio do you want reflected in the portfolio, and are you adopting a short-term or long-term approach?"

No portfolio checkup can be successful without an understanding of your current investment goals. Certain kinds of securities will probably be suitable for those who see safety as their chief aim, while others will be more appropriate for those who have a greater tolerance for risk. Some people may feel more comfortable with investments in local companies where they know the management, while others may prefer giant national corporations with a reputation for profitability and efficiency.

Whether your portfolio contains four stocks or forty, make certain at checkup time that it reflects your major concerns. Do you want to increase your current income? Do you want to reduce your tax liability? Do you want to hedge against inflation? Do you want to provide for retirement? You probably can't do all of the above, so your holdings should be in line with your most important objectives.

Since no portfolio is permanent, this recurring reevaluation of your holdings also should allow for external factors that may call for restructuring. Events in the worlds of finance, business, and government should be considered along with developments in your personal life.

Buy or sell decisions, for example, are bound to be influenced by major changes in federal tax laws, a substantial shift in the value of the dollar, or a significant weakening of international oil prices. And although most small investors can't appraise the daily effects of momentous economic events on their portfolios, they can try to gauge the impact whenever overall portfolio checkups are made.

"Once circumstances change, you may have to make a ninety-degree turn," says Randy Neumann, a certified financial planner in Saddle Brook, New Jersey. "You can't just pine away."

As Neumann sees it, "If you're running a portfolio, in a sense you're running a business, and you should have a hands-on management. Management by objective is a lot better than management by crisis or management by reaction."

Where to Start

How should a regular portfolio checkup be handled? Start by listing the current market price of your stocks, bonds, and other securities. These prices should be compared with your costs, taking account of withdrawals or deposits in the interim, in order to determine market performance. And the advance or decline percentage for each of these securities during the last year, quarter, or month, as well as for the portfolio as a whole, should then be calculated and compared against the record of one or more widely used market indexes—such as Standard & Poor's 500 Stock Index or the Dow Jones Industrial Average.

For many small investors, the next step—deciding when to sell—could be the hardest. An unemotional analysis of the performance of your holdings, and their relationship to the market as a whole, may indicate that a particular issue should be sold. And most individuals, regardless of the size of their portfolios and their experience in the market, are more inclined to buy or hold stocks than to sell them. Whether the value of an investment is up or down, the act of selling often represents a tearing away of something, and that is difficult for us to accept.

"Selling essentially involves making decisions that go against human emotions," says Robert Nurock, president of Investors Analysis, an investment advisory firm in Paoli, Pennsylvania. "But you should determine for each of your holdings a risk point or stop point—a time to evaluate whether to sell or not. Even for stocks that go up in value, you should constantly raise that point. You can't ignore something that's going wrong, otherwise a few losers can sometimes overwhelm a number of winners."

Furthermore, in contrast to financial institutions with millions of dollars' worth of holdings and the ability to diversify broadly, individual investors usually are limited to a small number of positions that could be severely damaged by a prolonged price decline. So it makes sense to determine your sensitivity to what portfolio managers call "the threshold of pain" and prepare to sell at least a portion of a position if the current market price falls by a specified amount—say, 25 percent—below your purchase price.

"Set a time period, such as two years, to meet a reasonable price objective," suggests Ben Niedermeyer, senior vice president of Janus Capital Corporation, the Denver-based investment advisor for the Janus Value Fund. "If it hasn't done so by that time, admit that you've made an error either on the fundamentals or on that security. And in the interest of keeping a portfolio fresh, get rid of that dead wood."

A predetermined holding period for stock market winners, as well as losers, is another possibility at checkup time. When your initial expectations regarding the performance of a security have come to fruition, it may be that the stock or bond has become fairly priced (or possibly overvalued) and the moment for selling may have arrived. A coolly intellectual approach here usually results in far greater profitability than emotional dependency on long-term ownership.

The final part of the portfolio checkup is reinvesting the money made available when securities are sold. But financial specialists warn that a snap investment judgment made primarily to put newly available funds to work quickly can be a costly mistake.

"Don't feel compelled to employ the proceeds from a sale too quickly," says Niedermeyer. "Let it sit idly in a money market fund, and wait until something attractive comes along."

Nurock of Investors Analysis agrees. "If you believe the stock market is going to continue to rise but the stocks you sold were fully valued, then go back to other stocks," he advises. "But if you believe that the stock market is at a peak, then go liquid, with Treasury bills and money market instruments, giving you safety and a competitive return until you get back to the market."

Some investors can do this analysis on their own, while others will need the aid of a stockbroker, financial planner, or accountant. But even if you engage a specialist to provide information, guidance, and recommendations, you still must come up with the facts and figures for the analysis and make the final decisions yourself.

"It's like taking a medicine that your doctor prescribes," says Isabel Francis Smith, a Birmingham, Michigan, certified financial planner. "The planner does the prescribing, but you have to take the responsibility and do something about it."

"I don't think anyone can have a portfolio checkup done successfully by someone else unless they are involved in what's going on," adds Nelson, the Cleveland lawyer. A portfolio checkup, regardless of how frequently performed, need not always be a lengthy exercise encompassing extensive market research and full-blown economic analysis. But it should be handled in such a way that when it is completed, you know what securities you now own, what their performance has been, and what alterations you intend to make in the period immediately ahead.

Your Portfolio List

To begin your portfolio checkup, make a list of all of the stocks and bonds you currently hold. Here is one convenient format:

	Stock/Bond	Cost	Price Now	% + or −	Planned Action
1.					
2.					
3.					
4.					

Checkup Checklist:
Ask Yourself These Ten Questions

1. Have my long-term goals changed since the last review of my holdings?
2. Do I have short-term objectives that I want to achieve with this porfolio, and are they being met?
3. Does my personal balance sheet show that I have sufficient cash and liquid assets to meet emergencies?
4. Will I change my job, my residence, or another key aspect of my life in the near future?
5. Is a major variation, either upward or downward, likely in my earnings over the next year?
6. Are any extraordinary expenses expected during the next year that would require me to sell securities?
7. Can I effectively swap stocks or bonds that generate taxable income for securities that yield a tax-free or tax-deferred return?
8. Are the holdings in my portfolio internally consistent and not overweighted in a single company or industry?
9. Can I acquire securities through programs offered by my employer that would have a major effect on the makeup of my portfolio?
10. Is my net worth increasing at a rate in keeping with my risk and comfort levels?

INVESTMENT STRATEGIES: SMOOTH SAILING IN ANY ECONOMIC WATERS

Economic conditions beyond your control have an effect on your financial security—especially when it comes to your investments.

In fact, your financial security could be badly battered if, for example, you leave your life savings stashed in fixed-return

CDs earning 7 percent, while inflation and interest rates range into the high double digits.

If nothing else, by refusing to shift your investment strategy to match the economic times you've missed out on a major money-making opportunity.

What are the various economic conditions that can help or hurt your portfolio, and what can you do to raise your profits or limit the damage?

For starters, see Table 6 on page 109. It shows how different investments have fared in periods of rapid inflation, disinflation and moderate inflation, price stability, and deflation. After glancing over the chart, come back here for tips on the right investment moves in each of these situations.

Rapid inflation. When the consumer price index is soaring, stocks occasionally do well—but not always. From 1949 to 1951, stocks returned (from dividends and appreciation) a healthy 24.8 percent a year. But more recently (1971 to 1981), stocks returned a paltry 5.8 percent.

Hard assets—housing, farmland, gold and silver—tend to do well in times of rapid inflation. Says Byron Wien, managing director and investments strategist (United States equities) at Morgan Stanley, "That's what *inflates.*"

Treasury bills and commercial paper perform adequately. Though, from 1971 to 1981, T-bills and commercial paper did exceptionally well. Reason: The 1970s saw the introduction and growth of money-market mutual funds (commercial paper), whose interest rates soared along with inflation.

Bonds do badly. The interest rates of older bonds seem paltry as inflation pushes up the rates of newer bonds, so the *value* of the old bonds sinks.

Let's say you buy a bond for $1,000 that pays 5 percent. When inflation hits, corporations will issue new bonds paying, say, 8 percent interest.

Let's suppose you want to sell your bond. Nobody with any sense would now want a $1,000 bond paying a mere 5 percent,

TABLE 6 ANNUAL RATES OF RETURN UNDER VARIOUS ECONOMIC CONDITIONS

	CPI+	Stocks	Bonds	U.S. T-Bills and Commercial Paper	Housing	Farmland	Gold	Silver
Deflation								
1871–1896	-1.5%	5.5%	6.4%	5.4%	N/AV	N/AV	*	-6.8%
1892–1895	-3.3	-2.5	5.1	4.1	1.5%	N/AV	*	-8.0
1919–1922	-2.0	5.0	4.2	6.7	1.0	-12.1%	*	-18.2
1929–1932	-6.4	-21.2	5.0	3.0	-3.9	-12.3	*	-19.8
Average	-3.3	-3.3	5.2	4.8	-0.4	-12.2		-13.2
Price Stability								
1896–1900	0.3	26.1	3.3	3.3	0.0	9.3	*	-1.0
1921–1929	-1.3	20.2	6.4	5.4	4.4	-2.8	*	-3.3
1934–1940	1.0	12.2	6.2	0.7	7.2	3.9	6.3%	1.0
1952–1955	0.3	24.5	3.5	1.5	4.5	6.5	*	2.1
Average	0.1	20.8	4.9	2.7	4.0	4.2		-0.3
Disinflation & Moderate Inflation								
1885–1892	0.0	4.5	4.4	5.1	N/AV	N/AV	*	-4.5
1899–1915	1.3	8.2	4.1	5.3	5.7	N/AV	*	-0.5
1942–1945	2.5	26.1	4.5	0.9	10.0	18.1	*	-3.3
1951–1965	1.6	16.5	2.2	3.5	5.5	6.7	*	3.0
Average	1.4	13.8	3.8	3.7	5.3	6.2		-1.3
1981–1985	3.8	20.2	22.0	9.6	5.3	-8.1	-0.5	-16.4
Rapid Inflation								
1914–1919	13.3	11.6	2.1	4.7	17.5	14.7	*	15.5
1940–1947	6.8	12.3	2.6	1.0	12.2	18.5	*	8.6
1949–1951	5.8	24.8	0.9	2.3	10.2	21.7	*	20.5
1965–1971	4.0	6.4	6.1	6.8	10.3	12.7	31.6	23.7
1971–1981	8.3	5.8	3.8	8.8	10.3	14.6	28.0	21.5
Average	8.3	12.2	3.1	4.7	12.1	16.4	11.9	18.0

+Consumer Price Index
*Under government regulation, the U.S. market price of gold did not change during this period.
Averages do not double count overlaps. N/AV = Not Available
Source: Morgan Stanley Research

so you must reduce the $1,000 down to the level where a buyer would get close to 8 percent on his or her investment. You would, in fact, have to sell the bond for around $625 (5 percent on $1,000 = $50; 8 percent on $625 = $50).

Lessons. If we are entering a period of rapid inflation, dump your bonds and replace them when inflation is at its peak—to lock in the astronomical yields being offered. Of course, it's hard to know when inflation *is* at its peak, so you might stagger your purchase of high-yielding bonds (or bank CDs which are also long-term debt instruments).

Meanwhile, bolster your hard assets. Have your home improved, or invest in more real estate via real estate investment trusts (REITs), real estate limited partnerships, mutual funds specializing in real estate stocks, or direct ownership. Consider buying gold and silver, perhaps through precious-metals mutual funds.

Stocks performed anemically in the 1970s' inflation spiral—probably because inflation was just *too* rapid. So these conditions *may* signal the need to prune out all but the bluest of your blue chips—the companies that dominate their markets, that can raise prices and rest assured that customers will still buy.

Disinflation and moderate inflation. If we are entering a period such as this, buy older, high-yielding bonds left over from inflationary times or newer bonds issued in the crossover period when rates are still high. You can either keep those bonds and enjoy unusually high interest, or sell them for a profit, once disinflation has clearly set in and all new-issue bonds are paying rates well below yours. For example, we are in a disinflationary time now, and if you had bought a crossover period bond paying 13 percent, you could sell it now for more than you paid for it.

Stocks also should do well: Companies are still selling their products and services at inflation-adjusted prices. And because interest rates in general are declining, stock dividends will look attractive—and stock prices should reflect this.

Gold and silver should decline, and housing may manage to hold its own. Keep your house, but consider surrendering your other hard assets.

Price stability. Stocks are far and away the best place to be. During tranquil economic times, stocks return an average of over 20 percent a year. Their nearest rival, bonds, return less than one quarter as much.

Deflation (or recession). When the consumer price index sinks, money becomes scarce. Interest rates, in general, go down. But if you have any old bonds, the corporations that issued them must continue paying the old, higher rates. Thus, if you bought a 5 percent bond that matures in thirty years, you would continue receiving 5 percent even during deflation—a robust return when the consumer price index (according to the chart) averages −3.3 percent a year.

Short-term instruments will also be desirable. Borrowers who need cash must pay relatively high interest to persuade you to lend them your money. But most other major investments, from stocks to real estate, will perform abysmally.

CAVEAT: Keep in mind that the relationship between the economy and the investments you should and should not buy is a fluid one. It is not etched in stone; on the contrary it can be upset by all sorts of variables. For example, while gold is generally considered a good investment during inflationary times, a political uprising in South Africa could flatten the gold market. History provides ample examples of broken investment rules: Stocks, which generally perform poorly in deflationary times, returned a healthy 5 percent between 1919 and 1922; 5.5 percent from 1871 to 1896. Housing, which tends to do well in periods of price stability, went nowhere from 1896 to 1900. Bonds supposedly do well during disinflation and moderate inflation, but from 1951 to 1965, they returned a paltry 2.2 percent.

Last lessons. As if you haven't heard it often enough, *diversify*. The economic climate can change quickly. If you have spread out your portfolio, you won't be caught (say fully invested in stocks during deflation, or mainly in bonds at a time of rapid inflation). During the inflationary 1970s, retirees relying mainly on fixed-income investments like bonds had a pitiful time trying to live within their means.

Finally, if you are not already in stocks (either individual stocks or stock mutual funds), seriously reconsider. As the chart indicates, over the years stocks tend to perform better than other major types of investments. In periods of price stability, disinflation/moderate inflation *and* rapid inflation, stocks typically keep well ahead of the consumer price index. (The period of 1971–81 is the exception that proves the rule. During that time, the CPI averaged 8.3 percent; stocks just 5.8 percent.)

Yes, the stock market is risky. Because of the market's gyrations, owning stocks can give you sleepless nights. But if you buy good stocks and hang on during the market's sometimes roller-coaster rides, you should do very well indeed.

HOW TO HANDLE ANY FINANCIAL EMERGENCY

Why do people who save money regularly, invest prudently, and scornfully resist screwball extravagances sometimes find themselves squashed flat by an avalanche of debt?

Typically, it seems, they're the victims of a double-whammy. One shock to their finances, they could probably withstand. Two shocks push them to the brink. And often one of those shocks is leaving a job, or putting a down payment on a house. Consider these cases:

◆ Carol Stevens, a journalist in Arlington, Virginia, was entitled to two months' paid maternity leave from her job. She decided to take three extra months, unpaid. She and her husband planned to meet their expenses during those three months by dipping into their $10,000 bank account. Unfortunately, the $10,000 was in a Maryland bank whose deposits were not federally insured. When the bank got into trouble, all its deposits were frozen—including Carol's. *Doublewhammy: her leaving her job plus the freezing of her savings.*

◆ A wealthy Houston family tax-deducted the money they had sent their elderly parents in Asia. But United States citizens can claim only people in this country, Mexico, and Canada as dependents. The IRS disallowed their deductions and demanded $5,000 in back taxes and interest within thirty days. The family had just put a $50,000 down payment on a house. *Double-whammy: owing taxes and being cash-poor.*

◆ A computer programmer in New Jersey quit his job to take a position in Pittsfield, Massachusetts, at double the salary. He carelessly let his company health insurance coverage lapse. On his first day at his new job he had a seizure, stemming from what was later diagnosed as an inoperable brain tumor. Before he died a year later, he had incurred over $100,000 in unreimbursed medical bills. *Double-whammy: not having health insurance and becoming very sick.*

How well you're protected against a financial crisis depends mainly on (1) whether you have enough insurance, and the right kind, and (2) whether you have enough cash reserves, and the right kind.

If you're caught in a crunch, your prognosis depends to a great extent on your levelheadedness. "My first advice to anyone in a financial crisis," says financial planner Lewis J. Altfest of New York City, "is: Don't panic."

Why Insurance Isn't Enough

Your first shield against such a cash crisis is insurance. At best, insurance can ward off unexpected financial catastrophes—everything from losing your job to a neighbor's suing you because he fell down your rickety stairs. (See "Insurance and Your Financial Security," page 120.)

But even if you're insured against most of life's slings and arrows, you might wind up in a financial crisis. Many insurance coverages have exclusions or limits. A health insurance policy may pay little or nothing for out-patient psychiatric care. Some basic homeowners policies will not reimburse you for damage caused by burst water pipes; most won't cover you for flood or earthquake damage, though you can buy special protection against these calamities.

Then, too, some emergencies are not covered by insurance policies. Your parents may become sick and need your financial assistance. Your child may be arrested and require top-flight legal help. You may be hit with a gigantic tax bill. You and your spouse may separate. Your grown daughter may be expecting, and her husband may have lost his job. The car you need for work may die an untimely death.

Certainly insurance is essential. But it may not be enough.

Cash for a Crunch

A second shield against a financial crisis is a cash-reserve fund. The conventional wisdom holds that a family should have an amount equal to three to six months of its yearly income, or at least its annual expenses, in such savings. The more insecure the breadwinners' jobs, or the more likely he and/or she would have trouble finding another, the larger the cash reserve should be. Obviously, someone who works for a gigantic corporation and receives all sorts of fringe benefits would need less of a cash reserve, proportionately, than a self-employed housepainter.

Whatever amount you decide on, you should be comfortable with it. That's the only real way of judging whether your cash reserve is adequate. You may want to adjust your reserve upward if your house and your marriage are not shipshape.

The assets in your cash reserve should be liquid—able to be turned into cash within a matter of days. They should also be stable as opposed to volatile; that is, whenever you decide to sell them, you can get a fair price. Interest-bearing checking accounts, savings accounts, and money market accounts and mutual funds all fit these criteria.

In contrast, while you might find someone to buy your house at a fair price right away, it's not a liquid asset. Getting money in exchange for the deed can take months. Stock that you own in a big corporation may be liquid, in that you could sell it in minutes, but the price might not be stable; if the whole stock market is down, your stock is probably in the doldrums, too.

Financial planner Altfest says, "I like cash. I like to see a good amount in a money market fund." But he also suggests putting part of a cash-reserve fund into three- and six-month CDs.

Richard W. Whitehead, a certified financial planner in Atlanta, Georgia, is more flexible. He would include shares in a mutual fund holding bonds, Treasuries, or quality growth and income stocks as part of a cash reserve, because "such funds are diversified and should remain relatively stable."

Another, although somewhat riskier, possibility is corporate- and municipal-bond, government, or Ginnie Mae mutual funds that allow check writing. Usually such checks must be for at least $250 or $500. While you shouldn't use such mutual funds as ordinary checking accounts, they certainly can provide quick cash in a pinch.

First Aid for Emergencies

If your financial pinch is relatively minor—say you don't have cash to fund this year's IRA or install a new furnace—all you may need is first aid.

Obviously, you can borrow from relatives. But be sure to borrow formally, giving them a signed note. Other forms of first aid: holding a garage sale, getting a salary advance from

your employer, cashing stock dividends you had been reinvesting, renting a room in your house.

You can also reduce spending by doing your own house repairs and maintenance, dispensing with your house cleaner, or
asking your creditors whether you can delay paying their bills.

That's what Carol Stevens and her husband did when their
$10,000 cash reserve was frozen. They delayed buying a new
car, ate less often in restaurants, postponed buying clothes,
watched more television and less theater. "We really scrimped,"
Carol recalls. "But when the baby was born, I didn't do the
diapers myself. I sent them out. I wasn't that desperate."

Two other ways of obtaining money to meet an emergency:

1. Borrow up to 95 percent of the cash value from any older
whole-life insurance policies you own. Policies issued fifteen or
more years ago charge only 5 to 6 percent interest; some issued as recently as seven years ago, 8 percent. Usually you
can get your hands on the money quickly, although some companies may stretch out the loan process as long as six months.
(Note: The money you borrow will reduce your current coverage. Interest payments are not deductible as a result of the
1986 tax reform law.) Some financial advisors think that borrowing the cash value in life insurance policies is a good idea,
emergency or no, providing that you use the money wisely.

The Houston family that owed the IRS $5,000 consulted Dallas
financial planner Jude R. L. Barcenas, who pointed out that
the cash value of their life insurance policies would amply cover
what they owed.

2. Scrutinize your assets for ugly weeds—poorly performing
stocks kept for emotional reasons or because you haven't re-
viewed your portfolio lately. Also consider cutting the flowers
that seem poised to fade—volatile stocks that have appreciated well beyond their usual price-earnings ratios and seem
heavily overpriced now. As for bonds, consider selling any whose
principal has eroded because the companies issuing them are
floundering. Where else can you get ready cash quickly?

You may be able to borrow the money you have invested in

a 401(k) retirement plan where you work. If you want to borrow more than $10,000, the limit is 50 percent of your balance, up to $50,000. The interest you must pay will vary (it is not tax-deductible). Usually you must repay the loan within five years; if it's for the purchase of a principal residence, you're allowed "a reasonable period of time," subject to interpretation by the IRS.

If you are an incorporated professional, you can borrow as much as 50 percent of your vested interest (up to $50,000) for as long as five years—and even longer if it's for housing. You'll have to pay a realistic interest rate on the loan.

You can also withdraw your money from any CDs you own. You must pay a penalty: a loss of at least one month's interest for a CD that matures in one year or less; a loss of at least three months' interest for a CD that matures in over a year. But paying the penalty may be less expensive than borrowing the money at a higher interest rate.

Another loan source: "margin," through brokerage houses. You usually must have at least $4,000 in securities in "street name" (the broker holds them), and the securities themselves must be sold on major exchanges (although you can borrow against over-the-counter stocks and mutual funds through some brokerage firms). You may be allowed to borrow up to 50 percent of the value of your stocks and convertible securities. Usually the interest rate will be lower than bank rates, and no time limit or repayment schedule is fixed to the loan. A brokerage house may lend you up to 70 percent of the value of your bonds, and up to 90 percent of the value of your Treasuries, but you should probably sell them instead—unless they return more than the interest you would pay on loans. But be aware if the value of the securities you've pledged as collateral declines sharply, you could receive a "margin call" to put up cash or additional securities.

If the emergency is brief and you regard yourself as disciplined, you might entertain a more risky tactic: withdrawing the money from your IRAs. You're allowed to remove that money once a year per account, keeping it for sixty days before rolling it over into another IRA account. If you wait longer than sixty days to return it, though, you'll owe a penalty and back taxes.

Sell or Borrow?

If your financial fix is so dire that you need a lot of money for a long time, consider "transfusions" (large loans), along with "surgery" (selling off valuable assets).

As a general rule, if given a choice between selling a valuable asset and borrowing, borrow. "Try not to disrupt a good investment program," urges one financial planner. Your assets may appreciate more than the interest you would pay, and—by serving as collateral for a loan—they would lower the interest rate you'd be charged.

You might also ask yourself: Are your stocks, bonds, real estate, gold, antiques, or other holdings high-priced now? If the answer is yes, consider selling.

Of course, in real life the decision whether to borrow more money, or to sell more assets, may boil down to how depressing it would be to sell your holdings—versus how nerve-wracking it would be to float a large loan.

If you decide on a loan, try not to borrow more than you can reasonably repay. Most people can easily cope with loan repayments amounting to 10 percent of their monthly take-home pay (not including a mortgage). They may have to scrimp if it's 15 percent, and have a terrible time if it's 20 percent.

One way to obtain a large sum of money cheaply is to refinance a high-interest mortgage. One of Altfest's clients owed the IRS $100,000. Luckily, he owned a house with a $360,000 mortgage at 15 percent interest. The house was now worth $600,000, so the $360,000 was only 60 percent of its value. The man wangled a new 10 percent mortgage for 80 percent of his home's value. That gave him $480,000 (minus closing costs), and the extra money covered his debts.

(Under the Tax Reform Act of 1986, you can still deduct interest on mortgages and other loans secured by your principal residence and a second home. But the deduction is limited to the interest on loan amounts up to the purchase price of the house plus improvements. There is, however, an exception for home-secured loans to pay for medical or education costs: This interest is deductible up to the market value minus other mortgages.)

Second mortgages, or home equity loans, can also be a good idea if you really need the money. Many banks and brokerage houses will even give you an open line of credit against the equity you have in a house—market value minus the mortgage. Usually a one-time application fee of one hundred dollars or so, and a yearly renewal fee of about thirty dollars, are required. But there also may be closing costs and "points"— one point equaling 1 percent of the value of the loan. These other costs may make a home equity loan more expensive than a loan with no collateral, so check carefully.

When the Clouds Clear

Once your cash emergency is over—the rain clouds are dispersing, the sun is breaking through—avoid the temptation to blot that nasty experience from your mind. Think about how you can prevent a recurrence.

Perhaps you need a larger cash-reserve fund. Perhaps you should chat about your insurance overage with both a knowledgeable life-health agent and a property-casualty agent. Perhaps what you need, most of all, is simply to save more and spend less in the future. Then again, perhaps you're already doing everything right—in which case you should be able to face any emergency with confidence.

Insurance and
Your Financial Security ◆◆◆◆

INSURANCE protects you against the unknown, those exasperating, often devastating events that come hurtling out of left field.

While a vital defensive element in anyone's financial armor, insurance can turn against you if you let it: Owning too much insurance is a common error and one that can actually weaken your financial position.

The challenge is to determine just how much insurance is enough. This section will help you make that critical calculation.

DISABILITY INSURANCE: A MUST

It's possible—perhaps probable—that you know how much life insurance you have and what the deductible is on your major medical insurance policy.

But do you have any idea how much disability insurance you have? Or if you have any at all?

If you're like most people, chances are that you don't know. The thought you've given to replacing your income if you become disabled runs a distant third to the consideration you've given medical and life insurance. Yet if you're under sixty-five years of age, the odds are far greater that you'll suffer a disability that will keep you away from work for more than three months than they are that you will die.

And the younger you are, the greater the odds. It is projected that 29 percent of people now age thirty will be disabled before they're sixty-five. For forty-year-olds the figure is 28 percent.

❖

You don't have to be a weekend sky diver or mountain climber to have a potential for disability. Even those who think they lead "safe" lives are open to risk. Consider the following hypothetical situations. Change the scenarios just a bit. Could any of these be you?

◆ On vacation at one of those lovely, multiactivity resorts, a rider mounts a horse for a few hours of trail riding. The horse stumbles on some loose rocks and the rider bounces out of the saddle. The most significant injury is a torn rotator cuff in his left shoulder. Although the injury does not require surgery, the rider, who earns his living as a sales representative for a clothing manufacturer, is in sufficient chronic pain to prevent him from driving a car to see accounts.

◆ An executive secretary to the president of a major corporation has been getting excruciating pains in her lower back. A physical examination reveals that she has a herniated disc in the lumbar region. Her doctor prescribes complete bed rest for two months in place of surgery and she is told to consider another line of work, since sitting is stressful on her back.

◆ On a Saturday morning trip to the store, a careful driver turns the car into the parking lot of a neighborhood shopping mall. In a split second the person is bumper-to-bumper with some jerk who didn't know the exit from the entrance. The careful driver winds up in the hospital with multiple internal and external injuries and is out of work for a total of four months.

◆ At a regular physical checkup, a patient complains of digestive problems. Three tests later, the problem is diagnosed as a malignant tumor in the colon. After surgery, the cancer patient must undergo debilitating chemotherapy for a year, limiting her participation as part owner and operator of a catering firm.

Assuming your medical bills would be covered by health and hospital insurance, you must assess what any of these illnesses or injuries might mean to you in terms of lost income if you were forced to slow down or abandon your occupation entirely.

Using Table 7 on pages 123–124, calculate how you would fare.

1. If you have 80 percent of your total monthly expenses covered at all stages of disability—immediately, after six months, after two years—you're in good shape financially. Less than 80 percent, and it's important to get additional personal coverage.

Cost is just one factor to consider when buying disability insurance. Other elements are equally if not more important.

2. Look for a "noncancelable" policy. Noncancelable means that the insurance company can neither cancel the policy nor change the rate.

"Guaranteed renewable" *sounds* as though it means the same thing, but it doesn't. Yes, the company must renew the policy—but not necessarily at the same premium rate. The insurance company cannot change the rate on your individual policy. But because it can change the rate for everyone in your class (all salespeople, for instance), the rate can continue to climb. The danger here is that you might find yourself priced out of the market.

3. The definition of disability offered in the policy is an important consideration.

"Inability to engage in your own occupation" means a person could engage in another form of work and still collect full or partial benefits. It's significantly better than "inability to engage in any occupation," a definition that allows you to collect benefits only if you can't work at all. Under the first and broader definition, a speech therapist who lost her hearing and was no longer able to do clinical work could author a text on the subject and still receive benefits.

4. Is the policy written to provide you with loss of income benefits if you are able to work, but on a reduced schedule? If not, can you obtain a rider at additional cost to cover this contingency?

TABLE 7 HOW WOULD YOU FARE FINANCIALLY IF DISABLED?

Monthly Expenses	Today	If Disabled
Mortgage (including property taxes) or rent	$_____	$_____
Utilities	$_____	$_____
Home repair and maintenance	$_____	$_____
Food and household supplies	$_____	$_____
Clothing	$_____	$_____
Insurance Auto, home, life, health (Do you have a waiver of premium on health and life?)	$_____	$_____
Credit card charge accounts and loan payments	$_____	$_____
Transportation	$_____	$_____
Medical and dental (unreimbursed)	$_____	$_____
Education	$_____	$_____
Other:		
Taxes (amortized)	$_____	$_____
Total Other	$_____	$_____
Total Monthly Expenses	$_____	$_____

TABLE 7 HOW WOULD YOU FARE FINANCIALLY IF DISABLED? (cont.)

Substitute Income If Disabled	Immediate Monthly Benefits	Monthly Benefits After 6 Months	After 2 Years
Group disability insurance (tax-free if you have paid premiums; taxable with an annual exemption of $5,200 if you haven't)	$_____	$_____	$_____
Social Security (Benefits for permanent or indefinite disabilities begin with the sixth month. Dependents also qualify for certain benefits. Call a Social Security office and ask what disability benefits you can get.)	$_____	$_____	$_____
State disability plans	$_____	$_____	$_____
Workers' Compensation	$_____	$_____	$_____
Veterans Administration	$_____	$_____	$_____
Personal disability insurance (remember: it's tax-free)	$_____	$_____	$_____
Spouse's income	$_____	$_____	$_____
Savings and investment income	$_____	$_____	$_____
Legal settlements because of disabling accident	$_____	$_____	$_____
Borrowed or withdrawn money (from life insurance, employee pension and related programs, savings, etc.)	$_____	$_____	$_____
Other	$_____	$_____	$_____
Total Monthly Substitute Income	$_____	$_____	$_____

Suppose an accountant has a heart attack. He or she can continue to work in the same field after the initial hospitalization, but—on doctor's order—must cut back on the number of hours spent working each day. Obviously, that means a loss of income. Would the accountant receive disability benefits proportionate to the loss of income, or would he have to forsake a return to work before payment was made?

5. Does a period of total disability have to precede a period of residual disability before benefits are paid?

That would be fine in the case of the accountant with the heart attack, but it would be disastrous for a person suffering from a degenerative disease such as multiple sclerosis or rheumatoid arthritis.

6. Does the payment of benefits depend on the cause of the disability?

Some companies distinguish between disability as a result of illness and disability as a result of accident—and this results in a difference of benefits payments.

7. How long will the benefits last? A year? Until age sixty-five? To age seventy-two if still employed full-time?

The answer to that question depends on the policy, what you need, and how much you're willing to pay in premiums.

8. How long can you wait before you need disability payments to begin?

It depends on your personal financial situation. The longer the waiting period, the lower the premium.

As is true with all insurance contracts, disability income insurance is based on the "what if." If you haven't asked yourself, "What if my income were to vanish?" now is the time.

THE FACTS OF LIFE (INSURANCE)

If you rated financial topics for glamour, excitement, and trendiness, life insurance probably would be number ten of ten.

But what it lacks in pizzazz, it makes up for in importance: Life insurance, for most of us, is essential—an indispensable way to give financial protection to those we love in case of our death.

Relying solely on an agent's pitch when purchasing life insurance is not enough. To get the best coverage for yourself and your family, follow this painless guide to life insurance:

Its prescription for buying smart is simple: (1) Buy it—only if you need it; (2) get the right dollar amount; (3) pick the right policy type; (4) compare costs to save. (Before proceeding, turn to page 139 and complete the "Five-Minute Estimate of Your Life Insurance Needs.")

1. Buy It—Only If You Need It

The only real reason to buy life insurance is if someone depends on your salary or services. If you have children under twenty-one, or you contribute substantially to your spouse's or parents' support, you probably need coverage.

On the other hand, if you're married, have no children, and you and your spouse earn roughly equal salaries, neither of you is likely to need life insurance. Your savings plus other liquid assets may be enough to cover the increased living costs of the survivor.

And odds are very high that you don't need coverage if you're single, with no financial responsibility for children or parents.

(None of this applies to purchasing life insurance for business needs—another story altogether.)

Not that some agents won't try to convince you otherwise. "Companies train insurance agents to discover needs (and sometimes create them if none exists)," points out chartered life underwriter (CLU) Robert W. MacDonald, former president of ITT Life Insurance Corporation, Plymouth, Minnesota.

So resist if an agent tries to push you to buy now for any of these reasons:

◆ To get a lower rate. It's true that the younger you are, the lower the cost of life insurance. "But does it make sense to buy something you don't need just because it's cheap?" asks James H. Hunt, director of the National Insurance Consumer Organization and former Vermont commissioner of insurance.

◆ To ensure your financial future. Advises MacDonald: "A better way is to get first-class health and disability insurance, develop a savings and investment program, and open an IRA." This is particularly so if you are young and just starting your career.

◆ To offset the risk that you'll become uninsurable later. You may, in fact, develop a condition that would disqualify you for standard life insurance rates later. But if you're in your twenties or early thirties, the odds of this happening are extremely low, says Hunt, who adds, "even if you should get sick, you still won't need life insurance if you don't have dependents. What you really need is disability income insurance to provide for yourself if you are unable to work."

2. Get the Right Dollar Amount

You should have enough coverage to bridge the gap between what your family will need and what resources it will have after your death.

On one side of the ledger, figure what costs your family will face: mortgage payments, payments on other loans, college expenses, everyday living expenses, and so on. On the other side, consider your spouse's income, employer-provided life insurance, liquid assets, potential pension benefits, and so forth.

Even if you have fixed in your mind an estimate of how much you need, it's still easy to be swayed into buying too much or too little insurance. In any case, make note of these tips:

More is not necessarily better. As you contemplate a "what if I die tomorrow?" scenario you may find you want more coverage than you need, just for the psychological comfort it will afford.

But splurging on life insurance may mean shortchanging your retirement fund. It doesn't make sense to overplan (and overpay) for the chance that you may die prematurely, and then underplan for the more likely possibility that you'll live to a ripe old age.

It's best to strike a balance: Buy adequate, but not excessive, death benefits (the amount of pure protection you get in a policy) and systematically accumulate assets to cover your retirement income needs. (As you'll see, it's possible to do both with certain types of policies.)

Less will leave your family vulnerable. Don't be deceived: Buying $75,000 of coverage when your family really needs $150,000 of protection ensures severe financial difficulties for your dependents if you should die.

And although it sounds unlikely, some agents will try to "sell you short." Why? So you can afford the policy that pays him or her the best commission. For instance, an agent may try to convince you to buy $75,000 of one type of insurance rather than $150,000 of another simply because the smaller policy sale will result in a larger commission.

3. Pick the Right Kind of Policy

For all practical purposes, there are only five basic types of coverage commonly sold today. And once you understand the concepts behind these five types, you will realize that every policy you come across is a simple variation on the same theme.

TERM INSURANCE

Best for you if: You simply want inexpensive, but solid life protection. It provides the most insurance for the lowest price and is the simplest, most straightforward type of policy sold.

How it works. Term provides sure protection, in the same way that car or fire insurance does.

You pay a premium to cover you for a specific period of time, usually a year or five years. If you die during that period, the face amount of the policy is paid to your beneficiary. If you survive the policy period, your coverage expires and the insurance company's financial obligations to you end.

Pros. It's cheap—especially if you don't have a large cash reserve, but do have people dependent on you for financial support. For example, $100,000 of term insurance could cost a thirty-five-year-old man (a nonsmoker) as little as $140 a year.

And although term insurance protects only for a limited time period, many policies now offer renewable clauses. Why is this so important (and positive)?

Let's say you become seriously ill. If you don't have the renewal option, the insurance company can insist that you take a new phsyical and then after seeing the results, simply decide not to take another chance on you. At that point, you may be hard pressed to find *any* insurance company to underwrite you. So, with all term policies, be sure the company guarantees in writing your option to renew—no matter what.

Cons. At the end of each renewable term, the premiums rise because your statistical chance of dying increases (you are, after all, older at the end of each term). The $100,000 of coverage that costs $140 at age thirty-five, may cost $210 at forty-five, $590 at fifty-five, and close to $1,600 at sixty-five. It may become too expensive to continue as your grow older. However, if you have been investing with an eye toward retirement, chances are that you won't need life insurance protection past your sixties.

WHOLE LIFE
(sometimes called straight life)

Best for you if: You have absolutely no risk tolerance or self-discipline when it comes to saving and investing. "Whole life is not a very cost-efficient way to create a nest egg for the future. But it is a sure thing in that the savings growth is guaranteed. And it is better than nothing, which is what some people would have if they didn't receive regular bills to force them to save, as they do with whole life," says Irwin W. Goldberg, CLU, senior consultant at Life Insurance Marketing and Research Association, Farmington, Connecticut.

How it works. Whole life, unlike term, provides you lifelong protection. Your premiums start high, but stay the same as you get older. The company, in effect, averages out the costs of carrying you over a lifetime by overcharging you when you're young and undercharging you when you're older. The premiums on a $100,000 whole-life policy, for example, might cost about $1,350 for a nonsmoking man when he's thirty-five, remaining the same when he's sixty-five years old.

Besides providing protection, a whole-life policy also builds a cash-value, an amount you can actually borrow from the company or redeem by cashing in your policy. The cash-value accumulation doesn't increase your death benefit—that remains constant—but it does accrue interest.

One breed of whole-life policy, called "participating," pays dividends. Whenever the actual cost of doing business turns out to be less than predicted, you get back some of your premium. When weighing the cost of a whole-life policy, check to see if the company has a history of dividend payouts in previous years, if dividend payouts are expected to increase over the years and if they will significantly offset the annual premium bill.

Pros. The interest you earn on your cash value is tax-deferred (and tax-free if you never withdraw it). Dividend payments are considered premium refunds by the IRS and therefore are not taxable.

A whole-life policy can provide a ready source of funds. And whole-life loans generally carry lower interest rates—today, about 8 percent—than loans available elsewhere.

Cons. You must make regular premium payments, or else your policy will lapse.

Outstanding loans are subtracted from the sum paid to your beneficiaries when you die.

How your premium dollar is divided among sales commissions, company overhead and profit, insurance reserve, and cash value is not disclosed in a whole-life policy. However, the insurance company will project the future growth of your cash value for you.

The interest rate credited to your cash value is generally far below prevailing market rates: Right now you'd get about 4–5 percent. Some companies, however, have begun to offer more competitive interest rates.

Finally, cash values build very slowly in the early years of the policy, then begin to mushroom only in the later years. That means if you cash in your policy after five years, you'll get very little in return for all those years of paying high premiums.

UNIVERSAL LIFE (UL)

Best for you if: You'd like a combination insurance/savings plan and you're somewhat flexible and self-directed when it comes to money matters. "Universal life is a better savings deal than whole life, and it's much less rigidly structured, which many people find it be a real plus," says David N. Becker, second vice president at Lincoln National Life Insurance Company, Fort Wayne, Indiana.

How it works. It's a combination of term insurance and a tax-deferred savings plan.

Your savings portion pays a flexible interest rate (9 percent is the going rate right now), but you're always guaranteed a minimum rate (usually 4 or 5 percent).

You can make premium payments at any time and in any amount after the initial payment. On a $100,000 policy for a thirty-five-year-old man (again, a nonsmoker), the minimum initial premium due would be about $800. If you don't regularly contribute to the policy, however, you have to be sure there's always enough in your savings portion to cover at least the cost of term insurance.

With UL you can also reduce or increase the amount of term coverage you have at any time—though increases generally require you to have another physical to prove you're insurable.

Pros. The savings element of UL generally builds at a faster, higher rate than the cash value of a whole-life policy. And as your savings grow, your coverage remains level.

The earned interest on your savings is tax-deferred.

You can make partial withdrawals from your savings, but you may pay a service charge of about twenty-five dollars per withdrawal.

You can usually borrow from your savings at just 2 percent net interest. How? If the insurance company charges you 8 percent on your loan, for example, it will generally credit your UL savings account with 6 percent interest on the borrowed amount.

UL's flexible premium feature lets you tailor your policy to fit your changing financial status. For instance, when you are short of cash to channel into savings, just keep enough in the policy to cover the cost of the term insurance.

On the other hand, if you have a windfall profit or receive a big end-of-the-year bonus, you can drop that lump sum into your policy. One possible benefit of making a big deposit: You won't have to pay premiums at all in the future. If money just remains within the policy, the accumulating interest may perpetually cover the cost of the term insurance.

The flexible death benefit allows you to reduce your coverage, easily and without charge—which you may want to do, for example, when your youngest child graduates from college. (When you amend a whole-life policy, you often have to change your entire policy, and take back savings.)

What's more, with UL you automatically get an annual report that spells out charges and fees, and shows you exactly how your premium dollar was doled out.

Cons. Your "target" premiums—the projected amount you must deposit to realize savings growth and cover the cost of term isurance—are based on the projected interest return, not on the minimum guaranteed rate. So if rates drop you may have to pay more to maintain your policy than you had initially anticipated.

Because of big initial fees and charges, your withdrawable savings won't amount to much unless you keep the policy for at least ten years. What you've saved on paper may be impressive, but you should always look at the policy's surrender value (the amount you can actually withdraw in cash) rather than its account value (the prepenalty or paper amount that's presently accumulating interest).

Term will cost you more within a UL policy than if you buy it outright.

With UL, you're not "forced" to save by regular bills, and if you open a UL policy, and don't use it to save, you'll end up with just a more expensive term policy.

VARIABLE LIFE (VL)

Best for you if: You need a tax shelter and are an experienced, risk-tolerant investor. "To manage a variable life policy properly—and profitably—you have to be well versed in equity investments. And you'll know whether you're well versed if you can comfortably read through the policy's complex prospectus," says Charles Woolley, vice president of marketing at John Hancock Variable Life Insurance Company.

How it works. Your death benefit has a guaranteed minimum, but goes up if your cash value increases.

VL's cash value is invested in stocks, bonds, money market funds, or any combination thereof—it's your choice. And you can move from one fund to another, or let the company's professional managers make such decisions for you. If your investment picks perform well, your cash value builds up. But you also risk reverses, and no minimum cash value is guaranteed.

VL premiums are fixed and level, and they are roughly equal to what you'd pay for whole life.

Like securities, VLs are sold only through prospectus, and salespeople must be registered with the National Association of Securities Dealers.

Pros. The potential gain on your cash value can be great if your investments do well.

The cash value can be divided so that the risk is spread among several kinds of investments. You also can shift or re-pattern your investment choices several times a year, usually free of charge. No capital gains taxes are due when you switch funds.

Any gains are tax-deferred.

You can borrow your cash value at competitive, or lower-than-market, rates.

Cons. You can forfeit your entire cash value if your chosen investment(s) perform poorly.

Partial withdrawals aren't advisable because cash withdrawals, in effect, mean rewriting your contract in a lesser amount.

You don't get reports showing how your *total* premium dollar is allocated, but you do get investment performance reports (and such publications as *Barron's* publish these regularly just as for mutual funds).

Your cash surrender value is small in the early years of the policy, because much of your premium goes to cover company expenses and fees. Consider VL a long-term, big-ticket commitment.

VARIABLE-UNIVERSAL LIFE (VUL)

Best for you if: You're comfortable with high-risk-reward investing and need significant tax-sheltering. "Variable-universal life is the best buy for the person interested in insurance with a more aggressive investment approach, because its fees and charges are relatively low," says Samuel H. Turner, president of Life Insurance Company of Richmond, Virginia.

How it works. It's exactly what it sounds like—a combination of variable and universal life insurance.

Like universal, you can vary your premium payments and change your death benefit.

The minimum premium due on VUL is roughly equal to what you would pay on UL.

Pros. You can hedge your bets by choosing different types of investments and change investment vehicles free of charge, twice a year.

There are no capital gains consequences when you switch investment vehicles.

Your gains are tax-deferred.

You can vary the frequency and amount of premium payments, even skip or stop payments altogether.

Partial withdrawals are possible, as are loans.

Coverage can be easily lowered to meet current insurance needs or raised, if you give proof of insurability.

You know exactly where every cent of your premium dollar goes, and you get monthly reports on the status of your investment as well as on policy transactions.

Cons. VULs are potentially risky—you could lose your entire premium investment.

Term insurance is generally costlier within VUL than outside it.

There are no fixed premium payments to force you to save or invest, should you need that incentive.

Although fees and charges in the early years are generally not as steep as with universal or variable, they're still significant—so you should plan on holding a VUL for at least seven to ten years.

4. Compare Costs to Save

There are no two ways about it: It pays to shop around. For example, $100,000 of universal life may cost a healthy thirty-five-year-old woman $650 in annual premiums at one company and over $1,000 at another.

So after you pick the policy type that seems best tailored to your needs, compare rates and policy features using the following guidelines.

IF YOU ARE BUYING TERM, COMPARE . . .

◆ First-year premiums, as well as those charged in following years, since some companies offer low entry rates, but relatively high renewal rates.
◆ Renewal provisions: How long will you be able to renew without proving insurability?
◆ Prices on plans similar to yours—from time to time.

For help, you might want to turn to Insurance Information. This computer information service will provide you with five or more competitive companies' term rates for a fee of fifty dollars. If the rates they come up with don't save you at least fifty dollars on the first-year premium, or if you find a better policy through another agent, your fifty-dollar fee is refunded. For more information, contact Insurance Information, Inc., 45 Palmer Street, Lowell, Massachusetts 01852.

IF YOU ARE BUYING WHOLE OR VARIABLE LIFE, COMPARE . . .

◆ Death benefits and annual premium payments.
◆ Guaranteed cash-value growth or projected investment yields after one year, three years, five years, seven years, ten years, and so on. Don't look at just the long-term gain, even though you intend to keep the policy for twenty years; statistics show that one person out of four drops his or her coverage within two years of buying it.
◆ Loan rates.
◆ How the annual dividends (if any) offset the premium costs.
◆ Cost-index numbers supplied by the insurance company (the smaller the index number, the lower the cost). But be wary of relying too heavily on these figures. Although ostensibly developed to help consumers comparison-shop, they can easily be manipulated to produce misleading results.

IF YOU ARE BUYING UNIVERSAL OR VUL, COMPARE . . .

◆ Interest rates or projected investment returns: Are they competitive with prevailing market rates?
◆ Premium payments: How are they calculated and what is the highest possible payment you may have to make to maintain your account?
◆ Cash surrender values: How much cash can you reasonably expect to get your hands on after one year, three years, five years, and so forth?
◆ Loan rates (and how interest is credited to your cash value during a lending period).
◆ One-time or first-year fees.
◆ Recurring fees (insurers deduct a percentage of all premium payments each year to cover company expenses and profits).
◆ Insurance costs: How much are you billed for term insurance?

Making a policy choice isn't easy, so it's comforting to know that you can always change your mind. Life insurance companies allow you ten days after you receive your policy—which may be weeks after your application—to return it for a full refund.

The Rule on Riders: Say No

Here are the four policy "extras" most commonly offered by life insurance companies—and four reasons not to opt for them.

Accidental death benefit (ADB). Also called double indemnity, it provides extra proceeds if you die of a "qualifying" accidental death.

It's hard to justify. Why should you provide more protection for your family if you die in a car accident than if you suddenly die of a heart attack? Also, it's costly and tricky to interpret (each insurance company's definition of "accidental death" is loaded with exclusions and exceptions).

Guaranteed insurability: Guarantees that you will be able to increase your coverage amount at standard rates without taking a physical.

It's an overrated, high-charge privilege, especially considering that it's available to you only when you're under forty.

Cost-of-living rider (COL): Lets you increase your coverage (without taking a physical) by an amount tied to changes in the cost of living.

Although they make sense in theory, COLs are overpriced because life insurance companies generally assume that only those in poor health will opt for the rider.

Waiver of premium (WP): Stipulates that the insurance company must pay your premiums if you become totally disabled. Because WP rates are on the steep side, you're better off buying disability income insurance, which would cover all your needs.

Trading Policies: Proceed with Caution

The new types of insurance policies have a lot going for them. You may be able to save a great deal of money as a result of lower premiums on your life coverage and higher yields on savings or cash value.

So consider replacing an old policy with a new one. Just keep the following in mind:

◆ Most new policies have two-year contestable and suicide clauses. This means that if you die within the first two years of owning the policy and any information on the application was falsified or if your death is considered a suicide, the death benefit will not be paid.
◆ Changing policies may require that you pass a new physical.
◆ A new cash-value policy will have a negative return for the first few years, since most of your initial premiums are used by the company to recoup its expenses in underwriting the policy and to pay the commission.
◆ New policies usually have higher loan rates than older ones.

◆ New policies usually mean a hefty first-year commission for the agent, so it's almost always financially beneficial for an agent to get you to switch. Never replace an old policy with a new one unless your agent will provide a replacement illustration in writing and will sign a statement saying that the replacement is to your financial advantage.

Tax Strategies

1. Don't make your spouse the owner of your life insurance policy; it's no longer a tax-planning strategy. That's because if your spouse is the beneficiary, all the death proceeds under your policy are paid to him or her free of estate and income tax—a result of the unlimited marital deduction. Consider your policy a tax shelter, since its cash value accrues tax-free.

2. If you have a universal or variable-universal policy and need money, you can withdraw the principal (the sum of your premium payments), which is not subject to any tax. If you need more money than that, don't withdraw the interest because you'll be taxed on it. Instead, borrow from the policy. Here's how it works. You pay about 8 percent interest to the insurance company, but the company credits your account with 6 percent. (It's like a savings account passbook loan, where your own money acts as collateral.) The tax implications:

◆ The money you've borrowed is not taxable to you because it's a loan.
◆ The 6 percent interest you are getting from the insurance company is tax-deferred (unless you surrender the policy).

The most this kind of loan can cost is a net 2 percent.

The Five-Minute Estimate
of Your Life Insurance Needs

No matter what your personal situation is, this test should give you a good estimate of how much life insurance you need—not want. If you do not have at least one dependent, don't take the test. You probably don't need life insurance. If any step is not applicable to you, enter 0 and continue.

1. You have at least one dependent _____
   you need to protect.   (name him or her here)
   Multiply your annual income by three .... $ _____

2. You named your spouse in step 1 because even though you earn equal or nearly equal wages, you have joint debts (mortgage, loans, etc.)
   Subtract one year's income .... $ _____

3. You named your spouse in step 1 because he or she cares for your children and doesn't earn wages.
   Add one year's income .... $ _____

4. You have children under eighteen years of age (other than and in addition to the dependent you named in step 1).
   Add one year's income for each .... $ _____

5. Your job provides group insurance.
   Subtract the amount of your group benefit $ _____

6. Someone other than your present spouse—such as an ex-spouse or parent—makes an equal contribution to the support of a dependent(s) (or would in the case of your death).
   Subtract two years' income .... $ _____

7. You have children between eighteen and twenty-three now attending or planning to attend college (other than and in addition to the dependent you named in step 1).
   Add one-half year's income for each ..... $ _____

8. Your dependent would, on your death, receive pension benefits or deferred compensation from work equal to or over a year's salary.
   Subtract one year's income .... $ _____

9. You have disabled children or children with special educational needs (include medical school, law school, etc.)
   Add one year's income for each .... $ _____

10. You expect to inherit money within the next three years.
Subtract the amount of your liquid assets $ _____

11. You own substantial *liquid* assets (stocks, bonds, savings, etc.).
Subtract the amount of your liquid assets $ _____

12. You have a dependent elderly parent, in addition to other dependents.
Add one year's income .... $ _____

13. Your Total Life Insurance Needs .... $ _____

What if the amount on line 13 doesn't seem to be enough? It doesn't reflect extras, only needs (enough, for instance, to help your child through college, but probably not enough to leave him or her a legacy).

If it seems to be too much, keep in mind that this one lump sum may have to support your family for many years to come. For example, $100,000 invested at 10 percent will generate only about $16,000 of compounded income per year for ten years.

**REMEMBER, IT'S TIME TO REEVALUATE
YOUR INSURANCE NEEDS IF YOU . . .**

◆ marry
◆ have children
◆ get a substantial raise
◆ buy a home
◆ begin caring for an aging parent
◆ divorce
◆ take out a substantial loan
◆ change jobs
◆ are graduating from college
◆ retire
◆ inherit money
◆ remarry
◆ make a windfall profit
◆ have a death in your family

PROTECTING YOUR HEALTH— AND WEALTH

Good health insurance coverage is one of the best ways to protect all your other assets. If you, your spouse, or child is struck by a prolonged illness and you don't have proper coverage, you could find all your resources drained by hefty medical bills.

As you grow older and require more frequent medical attention—if only for routine complaints—health care bills can mount quickly. Again, if you are inadequately insured, the damage to your financial security can be enormous.

How much health insurance do you need?

(1) You need insurance that protects you and your family against financially catastrophic illness or injury. Noncatastrophic medical expenses should be dealt with out of savings. (2) You need comprehensive coverage—insurance that pays no matter what the cause of illness.

Ideally your health insurance policy will provide a combination of basic hospital and major medical benefits.

Basic hospital usually includes hospital costs for a stated number of days, plus coverage for surgeons' and physicians' expenses. Major medical picks up where basic leaves off, paying for most types of care in or out of the hospital, with typical lifetime benefit maximums of $250,000 or $1 million. This is the coverage that protects you in the event of a catastrophic illness. As such, it is coverage you should not be without.

Should you opt for a $250,000 or a $1 million major medical ceiling? That depends on what you can afford and on your family's medical history. Does cancer or another serious illness run in your family? Do you have a son who rides a motorcycle or a daughter on the ski team? In short, how high are the health risks confronting your family? If you do choose the higher ceiling, you'll be pleased to find that the cost of increasing a policy limit from $250,000 to $1 million generally is not high, according to Charlotte Crenson, a Blue Cross/Blue Shield spokesperson.

New Health Insurance Guarantees

Until recently leaving a job under duress—because of a firing or layoff—or on your own initiative—to pursue self-employment or retirement, for example—often meant leaving behind affordable health insurance.

Some departing employees were offered the opportunity to convert group-rate insurance to individual coverage. However, premiums were often so high as to discourage this alternative. As a result, many people chose to go uninsured, leaving themselves open to massive financial loss in the event of a serious illness or injury.

Thanks to the Consolidated Omnibus Budget Reconciliation Act (COBRA) of 1986, however, these dangerous lapses in health insurance should become less frequent. The law guarantees an eighteen-month continuation of group health benefits to employees who leave their jobs *for any reason* other than gross misconduct (assuming they are not offered group coverage by a new employer and do not become eligible for Medicare). Benefits must be identical to those which you (and your family) received as an employee, and the cost may be no more than 2 percent above the regular group rate. That's a real boon to you since group insurance costs as much as 40 percent *less* than individual insurance you might purchase to replace group coverage.

The law also guarantees a thirty-six-month continuation of group health benefits to the dependents of covered employees who die; to divorced or legally separated spouses of covered employees; and to covered employees' children who cease to be dependents under the definitions of the group health plan.

The legislation applies to companies with twenty or more employees.

Getting Coverage Despite Illness

One of the worst side effects of a serious illness is the added difficulty of finding health, life, or disability insurance afterward. But it can be done.

For medical coverage. If poor health demands that you leave your job, you may have the opportunity to continue the same group coverage you had for an additional eighteen months by paying the full premium plus 2 percent—again, thanks to COBRA. This is also true for employees who are laid off.

After eighteen months, however, you must convert to an individual plan.

To make certain you're not converting to a plan that charges exorbitant fees, get a competitive bid. Try Blue Cross/Blue Shield.

Should you choose to get new insurance and not convert, know that of the Blues' seventy-six local plans, twenty-nine have periods when anyone can join; some are open for enrollment only one month per year, while others have continuous enrollment.

Like other insurers, the Blues may add a surcharge for an existing health problem or require a waiting period of six months to a year or more for preexisting conditions. Still, they rarely reject an applicant outright.

Another avenue to explore is group insurance available through professional, fraternal, religious, or alumni organizations. Membership may make you eligible, and it's possible that coverage could be more comprehensive and/or less expensive than coverage you buy on an individual basis.

For life coverage. There are companies that specialize in underwriting insurance for people with chronic or serious health conditions. To ferret out which company is best for you, find an independent insurance broker who handles hard-to-place cases. This person knows from experience which companies are more likely to insure people with specific conditions. Your regular broker can lead you to this specialist.

The bigger the life insurance policy you apply for, the more questions you're likely to be asked by the issuing company. So think of taking out several small policies, which can be obtained through a group plan from an organization you belong to.

Thanks to breakthroughs in drugs and medical technology, people who in the past would have been rejected out of hand by any insurance company, now have a chance of getting coverage, says Loy Fisel, director of life marketing support at Lincoln National Life Insurance Company, Fort Wayne, Indiana. "If people with kidney dysfunction take their medication, they can live normal lives—and sometimes even pay standard rates for insurance," he adds.

But the best advice about getting insurance is to get it when you're well.

Today's Health Care Revolution

Choosing a health care provider in today's world of proliferating choices is not easy: Health maintenance organizations (HMOs), preferred provider organizations (PPOs, a hybrid of traditional insurance plans and HMOs), urgent care centers, surgical centers, diagnostic centers, birthing centers—these are just a few of the new health care delivery systems that have gained prominence and considerable patient followings in the last ten years.

Why the popularity of these alternative health care centers?

For one thing, they are often less expensive than traditional fee-for-service physician and/or hospital care.

But selecting a health care provider solely on the basis of expense is a mistake akin to selecting a spouse on the basis of net worth: Both decisions can lead to dissatisfaction and even disaster.

Instead, when you face a health care decision, concern yourself with quality of care first; cost of care second.

Of the providers available to you, how can you determine

which offers the best quality for your health care dollar? Start by asking yourself these questions:

◆ Are you satisfied with your present health care provider? If not, which areas of service could be improved?
quality _____ physician availability _____
physician/staff attitude _____ cost _____
location _____ office hours _____.

◆ What is the current annual cost for medical insurance coverage for you and your family (estimate)? _____.

◆ What out-of-pocket (nonreimbursable) health care costs did you incur in 1987 (include insurance copayments and deductibles)? _____.

◆ Do you anticipate extraordinary medical expenses in 1988 (e.g., birth of a child, care of an aging relative)? If so, estimate cost through your current provider. _____

Now compare costs and quality of your current health care provider with comparable services offered through an alternative provider (e.g., HMO, PPO, ambulatory care center, etc.):

	Current Provider	Prospective Provider
What is your average cost per visit?	$_____	$_____
What is the cost for special procedures you are likely to require (e.g., ob/gyn, treatment of flu, infection, etc.)?	$_____	$_____
Does the facility meet licensing or accreditation requirements, if any?	$_____	$_____
What are the professional credentials of the physician(s) in charge?	_____	_____

	Current Provider	Prospective Provider
Is the provider affiliated with a hospital? If so, which one?	_____	_____
Must you use a plan-approved physician?	_____	_____
Do you see the same physician at each visit?	_____	_____
What are the hours of service and/or physician availability?	from_____	from_____
How long must you wait to schedule an appointment for nonemergency care?	_____	_____
How much time must you spend traveling to and from the office?	_____	_____
How much time must you spend in the waiting room?	_____	_____
Are you treated cordially and respectfully by the physician and staff?	yes_____ no_____	yes_____ no_____
Are your records centralized and easily accessible?	yes_____ no_____	yes_____ no_____
How do you pay for services rendered? —insurance claim form —cash/check at time of visit —charge card —billed for visit	_____ _____ _____ _____	_____ _____ _____ _____

HOW GOOD IS YOUR HOMEOWNERS POLICY?

Be it humble or grand, or mansion, your home and its contents are probably your most valuable possessions—and homeowners insurance one of your most important purchases.

The term *homeowners insurance*, in fact, may be misleading, because it does much more than protect your home and property. If a deliveryman is injured on your doorstep, your daughter's stereo disappears from her college dorm, your dog chews up a guest's fur coat, or your son breaks a neighbor's window, a homeowners policy can come to the rescue.

But all homeowners policies do not offer equal protection. When a loss occurs, it is painfully easy to find out too late that a small extra premium could have saved you a large sum of money. You also may be missing out on money-saving discounts that have come along in recent years.

"Most people just don't ask enough questions," says Steve Sanders, formerly with Metropolitan Property and Liability Insurance Company, Warwick, Rhode Island. "They could save money and aggravation if they did."

Here are eleven important questions to ask when you shop for new insurance or evaluate your present policy:

1. How do I determine how much insurance I need? The best figure to use in determining your insurance needs is the replacement value, the amount it would cost to rebuild, excluding land. Insurance companies or property appraisers can give you a fair estimate, usually based on local building costs per square foot. Bill Dommasch, homeowner division director of Geico Insurance, maintains that if you use the market value of your home you may be overinsuring if you live in an area where prices are highly inflated and underinsuring where prices are depressed.

Your minimum protection should be 80 percent of the cost of replacing your house, according to the National Insurance Consumer Organization (NICO) in Alexandria, Virginia, because most insurance companies will not pay in full even for partial damage with less coverage. Some mortgage lenders and many insurance companies actually insist that a house be insured for 100 percent of replacement cost. (Tip: If you choose 100 percent coverage, look for an additional guarantee ensuring full replacement even if the cost increases after the policy is written. Some policies include this, others charge extra.)

2. *Is my coverage "basic" or "broad"?* The most common *basic form* policy insures your house and its contents, shrubs and trees and outside structures such as a tool shed or garage, against eleven major hazards. They include damage from fire and lightning, windstorms and explosions, as well as that caused by planes or cars, vandalism and theft.

The *broad form* policy adds another seven hazards that are common enough to warrant consideration for most people. Among them are leaks from hot water systems, plumbing, heating or air conditioning, freezing of pipes; injury from faulty electrical wiring, falling objects, weight of ice, snow or sleet; and collapse of the building.

"Look for the broadest coverage for the dollar," suggests Thomas L. Vliet, personal property underwriting specialist for the Kemper Group in Long Grove, Illinois. One good choice might be the *special policy* offered by many companies. It gives broad coverage to the house but less extensive coverage on its contents, thereby holding down your premium.

But for maximum peace of mind, choose the *all risks* form, covering both house and property against all perils except those specifically excluded in all policies, such as flood, earthquake, war, or nuclear accident. "All risks" is the most expensive coverage but some policies make up for this in part by paying full costs in case of loss, without any deductible.

Separate insurance is necessary if you live where earthquakes or floods are a potential threat. If you qualify, the federal government offers coverage through the National Flood Insurance Program. (Phone 1-800-638-6620 for more information.) Earthquake protection must be obtained through private insurance companies.

3. In case of loss, will I be paid on a cost or replacement basis? It can be a rude shock to file a claim only to learn that policies that promise "actual cash value" are actually referring to your original cost *minus* depreciation over years of use. Home repairs at "actual cash value" may deduct enough for wear and tear on high-ticket items such as roofs, flooring, and siding to leave you footing much of the bill. Personal property can lose even more value. "A ten-year-old TV set will be worth almost nothing after depreciation," Vliet points out. "To cover a new set, you must have replacement cost coverage, which is based on the cost of a comparable set today."

On a home insured for $125,000, changing the policy from cash value to replacement value coverage averages around $50 a year, and can save many times that amount.

4. Will my most valuable possessions be covered? Most standard policies insure personal property for a total of 50 percent of the coverage on the house, meaning that $75,000 for the house allows $37,500 for its contents. An inventory of your personal belongings at today's prices will tell you whether you have sufficient coverage. You may be surprised to realize how much it would cost to replace your personal property.

An inventory, with your original cost noted, is also a great help in establishing claims in case of loss. Always save purchase receipts on large items such as appliances or home computers. Photographs of rooms and special belongings are helpful as well in case of loss, to establish your claim without any doubts. The Insurance Information Institute recommends keeping copies of your inventory and photos in a safe place away from home.

Most policies place a limit (normally from $500 to $2,500) on the amount they will pay for certain items such as jewelry, furs, or silver. To protect these valuables, you'll need supplementary insurance, called a "floater" policy, for the full value of each named item. Jewelry floaters average $0.30 per $100 of coverage if the items are stored in a safe-deposit box. If they're stored elsewhere, they can cost from $0.85 cents to $2.45 per $100 of coverage.

One other reminder from NICO. If you rent your home to others, don't assume everything is covered. Check with the company.

5. *Am I covered for personal belongings stolen or lost away from my home?* Your own and your family's possessions generally are covered, but the total amount of coverage is limited. Property lost at a secondary residence, such as stereo equipment taken from a college student's room, will be reimbursed up to a limit of 10 percent of the parents' personal property coverage. Thus, for the $75,000 home with a $37,500 property coverage, the amount paid for the loss at the secondary residence would be $3,750 with special limits on specific items. So items more expensive than the limit should be covered by a separate floater.

6. *Will I be paid for living expenses if I must stay elsewhere while my home is being repaired?* Policies pay the difference between normal living expenses and the cost of living elsewhere, not full living costs. Some set maximum dollar limits, commonly 20 percent of your total coverage, others impose time limits such as six or nine months.

7. *How much liability coverage do I need?* "Some people don't carry adequate liability insurance because they don't think good neighbors or friends would ever sue. The truth is they often do," says Myra West-Allen of Allstate Insurance, in Northbrook, Illinois. The liability portion of a homeowners policy is important. It covers everyone in the family, including Fido, for personal injury or property damage to others due to negligence on or off the premises. That can mean anything from beaning someone on the golf course to having a salesman trip over the garden hose.

It also covers medical expenses resulting from certain injuries, and the cost of legal defense if you are sued. Generally, basic coverage allows $100,000 for liability insurance and $1,000 for medical expenses. But you should review your policy with your agent to be sure your level of protection is adequate for where you live. (For more on liability insurance, see page 154.)

8. What kind of insurance do I need if I live in an apartment or condominium? Special policies for apartment renters and condo owners protect possessions from theft or fire and provide liability coverage. Condo policies also insure permanent additions or improvements that have been added, such as built-in cabinets or shelves. These policies are relatively inexpensive since they do not have to cover the structure itself. In the case of condos, a master policy, taken out by the condominium association, should cover the basic structure and common areas.

9. What are the best ways to save money on homeowners insurance? Substantial savings are achieved if you share some risk with the insurance company by accepting a higher deductible. Premiums usually go down around 10 percent if you accept a $250 deductible instead of the usual $100. They can be further reduced if you up the deductible to $500.

Recently companies have instituted discounts for clients who make their homes more secure from theft or fire. By installing dead-bolt locks, smoke detectors, and fire extinguishers, you may be able to cut premiums as much as 5 percent. Installing a basic burglar alarm can be worth 2 percent, while an alarm connected to the local police or fire department may mean savings of 3 to 5 percent. A burglar alarm hooked to a central monitoring station rates a 5–10 percent cut, and if a fire alarm is added, the discount doubles.

Some companies also have discounts for nonsmokers, for houses under six years old, and even for retired homeowners who stay at home and are therefore less likely to be burgled. Some companies also offer more favorable rates for those who use them for both auto and homeowners insurance. Discounts vary by company and by state, since each state has its own insurance regulations.

10. How often should I review my insurance? A practical timetable is at least once a year, to make sure your coverage is keeping pace with inflation. While most companies offer automatic inflation protection that increases the amount of coverage each year, it's a good idea to review the increase carefully, especially if prices in your particular area seem to be escalating more quickly than elsewhere.

Too many people renew without giving these considerations much thought, says Mary Zavada of the Insurance Information Institute. "If you put an addition on your home, buy a home computer or expensive new jewelry, these should be added to your policy," she says. Also don't throw away the enclosures that come with your renewal without reading them: They may be informing you of newly declared discounts that can save you money.

11. Do I need an insurance agent? A good agent can definitely help. He or she should have computerized rates available to quickly compare different offerings. If the broker does a lot of business with a specific company, he or she will also get preferred rates, which can save you as much as 20 percent.

How to pick an agent? "First look at the companies the agent represents," suggests Albert H. Lewis of Lewis and Associates in Stamford, Connecticut. "Be sure they are reputable companies. Then see how long the agent has been in business. Years of experience mean knowledge that is valuable to you. Find out how long the agent has represented specific companies, as well. That will tell you whether he or she is likely to have clout with them if you have problems."

Know, too, that there are companies known as "direct writers" who either do not use agents or employ their own agents, sometimes passing on saved commissions to customers in the form of lower rates. These insurers are most competitive in the areas where they do their most substantial business.

A broker will not always recommend the cheapest policy, however, and you should not always take it, advises Lewis. "Most companies are competitive," he points out, "and rates are within ten percent of each other. What matters far more is the company's reliability, whether they pay promptly and fairly, whether they come through when you need them."

LIABILITY INSURANCE: HOW MUCH IS ENOUGH?

Twenty years ago, you probably wouldn't have considered suing the family doctor. Now you might not think twice about filing a malpractice suit. It works the other way, too. If a neighbor tripped on your sidewalk a few years ago and wasn't hurt, you might never have heard about the accident. Today, the first hint of trouble could be a million-dollar suit claiming negligence, medical expenses, lost wages, and pain and suffering.

How much liability coverage is enough in our increasingly litigious society? "You need a lot more coverage than you used to," says Harvey Seymour, spokesperson for the Insurance Information Institute, an insurance industry group. In 1962, there was a single million-dollar liability verdict award in the United States, according to Jury Verdict Research, an analysis firm in Solon, Ohio. In 1982, there were 251. In 1985, the Insurance Information Institute counted 401 million-dollar-plus awards.

Most of us already have liability protection through homeowners (or renters) and auto insurance. The good news is personal liability insurance covers almost any event that is not job-related (you need a separate policy for business/professional liability). You can expect coverage of all damage and expenses for which you are held legally liable, including medical payments. Most policies also cover damage and expenses for which you are not responsible but in which you were involved. Coverage usually follows you anywhere in the world.

But this basic coverage can fall far short of actual needs. Standard homeowner policies offer as little as $100,000 in personal liability coverage. Auto liability protection, even in states which require it, can be as low as $15,000 per person per accident, $30,000 for two or more people, and $5,000 for property damage.

There are no firm rules on how much liability coverage is enough, says Everett Brookhart, chief of consumer affairs for the California State Department of Insurance. "It's a very personal question," he explains. "You have to look at what you can afford to pay and what assets you want to protect."

Brookhart and Seymour suggest carrying at least enough liability coverage to protect your net worth. If you're particularly successful or visible in your community, you may want to increase coverage to the market value of major assets, such as home and investment portfolio, because you are more likely to be sued and more likely to be hit with higher damage awards.

How much does liability protection cost? Liability rates vary from company to company and state to state. It may be cheaper to increase coverage with a $1 million (or more) umbrella policy than to up the limits on existing homeowners and auto policies. You can expect to pay $150 to $200 a year for a $1 million umbrella policy in most areas.

One way to minimize the net cost of personal liability protection is to raise the deductible on your ordinary homeowners and auto insurance, then apply the savings to an umbrella policy. Raising your homeowners deductible from $250 to $500, says Seymour, should save $50 to $60 a year, one-quarter to one-third the cost of a $1 million umbrella policy.

INSURANCE YOU DON'T NEED

Would you buy insurance that pays for a pet's pacemaker? Or a policy that pays off if the sun doesn't shine on your vacation?

How about one that pays for lost contact lenses?

Those are only three of the many specialty insurance policies offered today. They're also three policies that you probably don't need.

Americans spend 12 percent of disposable income on insurance. Robert Hunter, a former federal insurance administrator and now president of the private National Insurance Consumer Organization in Alexandria, Virginia, thinks that's too much. The only reasonable insurance purchases, he says, are life, disability, health, auto, and home. NICO calls limited policies that protect against a single disease or event "junk insurance."

"You should buy comprehensively to cover against catastrophic losses," Hunter explains. In other words, *comprehensive* for a broad range of coverage, not a tiny slice of protection; *catastrophic* for economic disaster, not temporary inconvenience.

Insurance against being mugged, fired, squashed by a falling satellite, taken by a con artist, audited by the IRS, or attacked by extraterrestrials are only some of the more unusual policies available. Here are a few of the more popular specialty policies you're probably better off without.

Cancer insurance. Former TV host Marlin Perkins and his wife starred in an ad campaign with the theme "Cancer wasn't the end of our world." The couple was pitching cancer insurance that paid $2,500 upon diagnosis of internal cancer and up to $150,000 for treatment.

The policy could be a good deal if you get cancer, but a comprehensive medical policy would be even better. Cancer policies are limited. Secondary problems or nonhospital care and expenses may not be covered. And if you end up with heart disease, which is far more common than cancer, the specialty policy won't pay off at all.

"That should all be covered in a comprehensive policy," says Wayne Cotter of the New York State Insurance Department. He adds that cancer and other specific disease policies offer so little protection that New York State generally prohibits their sale.

Children's life insurance. The only reason to buy life insurance is to protect survivors should *the* breadwinner or *a* breadwinner die. Parents who buy life insurance on their children are wasting money unless the children produce a major portion of the family income. "Under most circumstances," says Cotter, "we don't feel it's a wise idea" to insure children. The death of a child can be emotionally devastating, but it is rarely a financial crisis.

Contact lens insurance. A policy that covers loss or damage to contact lenses typically costs $25 for one year or $48 for two years, plus generally an $8 to $12 deductible. Contact lenses can be purchased for as little as $25 each in most major cities. At that price, you could replace a set of contacts every other year for less than the cost of the insurance and deductible.

Flight insurance. Life insurance offers more comprehensive protection for air travelers than flight insurance does. Even though 1985 was the worst year on record for air crashes, there were fewer than three deaths per *billion* passenger miles. Air travel is still the safest way to go almost anywhere, and flight insurance (fortunately) is a surer loser than any bet Las Vegas or Atlantic City can offer.

Then there's the cost. A major insurer recently offered a $150,000 flight insurance policy for $5. If the whole trip takes ten hours, including travel to and from the airport, you're paying an annualized premium of $4,380. That's twenty times the premium a healthy forty-year-old male airline pilot would pay for a $150,000 term life insurance policy that covers death at any time, not just while traveling by air.

The only bargain in flight insurance is the free coverage offered by credit card companies such as American Express when tickets are charged on their card.

Moving insurance. Losing a truckload of household goods could be an economic disaster, but moving insurance is riddled with loopholes. Do-it-yourselfers, who need the most coverage, generally get the least protection. Cargo insurance often excludes exactly the damage you'd most expect it to cover. Losses from breakage, marring, scratching, and wetness aren't covered under many circumstances. If furniture is damaged as the truck swerves to an unexpected ramp, you may not be covered.

Fortunately, many homeowners' and renters' policies cover household goods in transit. To increase the amount of coverage, or to cover all risks during a move, Cotter suggests buying a rider for an existing policy. "All risk" insurance purchased from the moving company will probably cost more and include a requirement that company employees do all packing and unpacking—at standard hourly rates.

Pet medical insurance. All catastrophes are not equal. Many people consider health insurance for their animals at least as important as their own coverage. Veterinarians don't sell pet medical coverage, but several companies offer accident and major insurance for dogs and cats (other domestic animals aren't yet covered).

The typical policy costs between $24 and $99 per year, depending on the animal's age, and pays up to $750 per "incident." Hunter suggests that vets who recommend pet medical coverage are more interested in selling expensive treatments than in protecting pets.

Rental car insurance. Car rental companies have been steadily raising renters' liability for repairs and the premiums to cover the liability. The coverage is called a collision damage waiver (CDW). In 1971, the average CDW cost $2 per day, and without it, renters were liable for the first $100 in repairs. In 1985, Hertz, to cite one example, increased its CDW from $6.95 to $7.95 a day and the limit of liability without it from $2,500 to $3,000.

Rental counter personnel commonly use dire warnings of liability to pressure customers into accepting CDWs. Their employers may rake in more than $1 billion a year in premiums to pay for actual repairs.

What they don't explain is that many auto insurance policies already include collision and comprehensive coverage for rental cars. Coverage and deductibles vary from policy to policy and state to state, so check with your insurance agent before renting a car.

Vacation insurance. Several companies offer policies that guarantee sunshine in a specific location on specific days. If the weather is bad, you get your vacation expenses back. But while bad weather at vacation time may be an inconvenience, it's seldom a disaster. And if it isn't a disaster, it isn't worth insuring in the first place.

Financial Security
and Your Career ◆◆◆◆

WITHOUT a job, a steady paycheck, and employee benefits, financial security would be unattainable for most of us.

That's why making the most of this fundamental income stream with smart career moves is so important.

If you are a million-dollar lottery winner, or are living comfortably on inherited wealth, this section is not for you. Ditto for the self-employed.

But for everyone else who would like to turn their jobs into a greater source of financial security, read on.

THE BEST AND THE BRIGHTEST JOBS

Where can you find ample employment opportunities and salaries that go beyond the norm—to the positively smashing in some cases?

John W. Wright, author of *The American Almanac of Jobs and Salaries,* has identified six fields that are experiencing extraordinary growth. According to government estimates, attractive jobs will be plentiful in these fields through 1995 or 2000:

1. Computer technology. By 1990, there will be a near-50-percent increase in jobs that require computer skills; as many as 685 new jobs may become available. Even better, many of those jobs will pay extremely well. A college graduate with a B.A. in computer science may command $28,000 to $30,000 in a first job as a systems analyst, Wright says. At the very top end of the pay scale, the heads of data processing departments in major corporations earn as much as $175,000 annually in salary and bonuses.

2. Health care. Life expectancy is up, the birth rate is down, and that equation translates into an increasingly large elderly population *and* a greater need for health care workers. The government projects 500,000 new nursing jobs (salary range: $15,000 to $34,000) before the turn of the century. There is also a strong demand for physical therapists (average starting salary, $20,000; with ten years' experience, over $40,000), health care administrators ($40,000 to $150,000), and psychiatrists (average annual earnings, $85,000). The latter profession is on the upswing owing to advances in medically based treatment of psychological illness and to the rise of rehabilitation centers for substance abusers, Wright notes.

3. Engineering. "If we are going to continue to develop and compete in the world economy, we need more engineers," Wright explains. Right now, the demand in many disciplines for newly graduated engineers is above average. That's one reason that beginners' salaries are attractive—in the $23,000 to $32,000 range. After five years, engineers typically earn $33,000 to $40,000 a year. Salaries climb upward from there, depending on education level and performance, but engineers seldom crack the $80,000 mark, and almost never reach $100,000. This is one profession where salaries stall out early, says Wright, especially if you show little aptitude for supervisory roles.

4. Human resources. People in this field (also known as Personnel) "are very much at the hub of activities and the future of today's corporation," says Wright. Responsibilities include recruiting and hiring at all levels and the administration of employee benefits and labor policies. In general, salaries in human resources have been increasing at better than 10 percent a year for the past few years, Wright notes in his book, and the future looks very promising, with job openings expected to increase by almost 20 percent over the next decade. Salaries range from $14,000 for clerks to $150,000 for vice presidents of large corporations.

5. *Accounting/finance.* An ongoing rash of mergers and acquisitions, a tremendous amount of new business formation, as well as the 1986 tax overhaul are fueling the already considerable demand for finance professionals, says Wright. Accountants' salaries range from $18,000 on the low end to about $65,000. *Women take note:* The Robert Half Agency has found that women accountants are easier to place than men. In fact, women were chosen over men three times out of four for one hundred different accounting jobs paying between $15,000 and $50,000.

6. *Sales and marketing.* This field offers good first-job opportunities for college graduates. Especially for those with technical backgrounds—in aerospace or electronics, for example—salaries can be enticing, starting at $30,000-plus and ranging to $50,000. For salespeople in nontechnical fields, average earnings for trainees are $20,000; $30,000 for semiexperienced salespeople and $37,000 for fully experienced salespeople. Marketing personnel within corporations now have a lot of clout, notes Wright, *and* the ability to scale the high echelons of the salary structure.

CHECKING OUT A PROSPECTIVE EMPLOYER

After three interviews, you get an offer: big salary, bonuses, the works. The company looks great; you want to say yes. But you're concerned your new firm isn't as healthy as it seems. How can you find out what financial shape a company is in?

Ask for financial statements. "Balance sheets and income statements for the past five years should be available whether the company is public or private," says Charles Brandes, a securities analyst in Del Mar, California. "If the financial reports are audited, great. If not, that's still okay."

When you do get the reports, what should you or a CPA look for? Andrew McCuen, a San Diego-based certified public accountant, zeroes in on payables and receivables: "If payables are going up relative to receivables and cash, that means the company isn't paying its bills," he says. But you should also look for long-term growth in sales, and sufficient cash flow to cover your paycheck easily.

Go to Standard & Poor's, Moody's, or Value Line. For public companies, expect to find financial information and hope to find a healthy and growing net income and net worth.

Check with Dun & Bradstreet—especially for privately owned companies. Kathy Fowler, of D&B credit services, explains that while an individual can't belong to D&B, you *can* ask prospective employers to produce a "self-inquiry" for you. This gives financial and credit information, verified by D&B. If you can't get that, simply ask what the company's D&B credit rating is. D&B will tell you that rating as an alphabetic code and explain the code—all over the phone.

Get a commitment. If you're hired for a specific project, make certain that if the company loses that project you'll stay on in a different capacity. A company is far more likely to lose an account or two than to go under completely.

And no matter where you go, when you depart your current job, always leave a door open—just in case.

DON'T FORGET EMPLOYEE BENEFITS

It happens again and again: A prospective employee is so blinded by a job offer and enticing salary that he or she fails to evaluate the package of employee benefits the new employer has to offer.

This omission can be critical, because benefits represent a

significant portion of the typical employee compensation package. Think of it this way: If you had to pay the full cost of your health, life and disability insurance, and fully fund a pension plan, you'd be out a lot of money. Other employee benefits, such as thrift plans or employee stock option programs, make saving and investing easier and more profitable; thus they represent additional income to you.

Seeking out and/or negotiating for the best possible benefits package should be one element of your job search.

The benefits you deem most valuable will vary according to your age, income bracket, and family circumstances. Your accountant or other financial advisor can counsel you on the relative merits of a defined benefit or defined contribution benefit plan, for example, or determine whether a 401(k) plan would be of considerable value to you.

Though it's impossible to rank benefits in order of importance, you may be interested to know which benefits cost your employer the most to provide. (It's one way of gauging how much the benefits are worth to you.) This list, compiled by the Employee Benefits Research Institute, tells the story. Benefits are listed in descending order, from most to least expensive:

1. Pay for time not worked (vacations, holidays, sick leaves).
2. Retirement benefits (pensions and profit-sharing plans).
3. Health insurance.
4. Short- and long-term disability insurance.
5. Group life insurance.
6. Thrift plans.

SUREFIRE STRATEGIES FOR GETTING A RAISE

When your morale, not to mention your sense of financial well-being, is flagging, nothing works like a big fat raise to buoy your bank account and send your confidence soaring.

Your annual performance review is just one opportunity for scoring a salary increase. Other chances are likely to come your way. If you're alert to them and act decisively, your actions will surely lead you to a position of greater financial security.

How can you get the raise you feel you deserve?

We solicited the advice of ten recognized career experts. Here's what they have to say about your best strategies for landing a juicy raise in five distinct job situations.

Situation 1

Your boss just approached you with a special assignment—to develop plans for a new division. It's a plum project, one you've been hoping for. *But* you'll have to work many late nights and weekends to complete the job in the allotted period of time. You feel you should be compensated for the extra work, but, because you're in a managerial position, you receive no overtime pay.

How should you go about requesting additional compensation?

Successful completion of this plum assignment definitely deserves some form of compensation, agree our ten experts, but there's less unanimity about what kind of compensation to request and how to go about getting it.

"You have the best shot at getting money through job redesign," advises Marilyn Moats Kennedy, author of *Salary Strategies: Everything You Need to Know to Get the Salary You Want.* She suggests you begin the project and, at the same time, rewrite your job description for a higher salary-level position. "As soon as you have positive results to show, go to your boss with your proposal and your request for a raise."

Nella Barkley and John C. Crystal, of the John C. Crystal Center for Creative Life/Work Planning in New York City, also favor job redesign, but warn against asking for compensation before completing the project. "This assignment is an expression of confidence in your professionalism, and a clear indication that you're being considered for better things," they explain.

"If your first reaction indicates you equate your time only with extra dollars, this crucial aura of executive professionalism will be dispelled quickly."

Instead, they suggest, draw up a proposal for the new division, including your normal work and new responsibilities. When you discuss the plan with your boss, be sure to request an appraisal of your performance once the assignment is completed. When the appraisal comes in—assuming it's positive—that's the time to ask for a raise.

John Ilich, who wrote *Power Negotiating: Strategies for Winning in Life and Business,* says you should assess your negotiating position before making a move, and do whatever possible to strengthen it. If you determine that you were given the plum project because you're the most qualified employee, and if you know your boss well enough to gauge his or her response to a raise request, your negotiating position is strong.

Discuss all aspects of the assignment with your boss so he or she knows exactly how much extra work it will entail. This increases your negotiating leverage, Ilich explains. Then, he says, "get an informal agreement that you'll receive additional compensation *after* successful completion of the project."

Steve Kravette, author of *Get a Raise in 60 Days,* suggests a variation on this plan: "Assure your boss you'll jump in and play out the project full tilt; he or she can count on you 100 percent. Also assure your boss that if your results are even 75 percent as good as you believe they will be, you intend to ask for a raise that will reward your efforts appropriately." That way, explains Kravette, "management will be ready for you when you ask."

Several experts point out that a raise is not the only, and perhaps not the best, option for compensation. Other "perks," like additional expense account money or vacation time, for example, or added life or health insurance, may be easier to get and *do* show that management wants you enough to keep you happy. You may request perks to tide you over until a raise is possible, or as full compensation for the special project. In either case, nontaxable perks are worth money to you now.

Situation 2

You have heard from a business acquaintance who holds the same title as you elsewhere in your company, and who started in this position at the same time you began yours, that he or she earns $5,000 a year more than you do.

How do you go about using this information to secure a raise for yourself?

There is unanimous agreement here: Before doing anything, collect more facts. "Taking any action based on one isolated piece of information is naive and ineffectual," warns David J. McGlaughlin, who wrote *The Executive Money Map*.

First, determine if the two jobs really are equivalent, Barkley and Crystal advise. If you have the same title as your acquaintance but are in charge of fewer people and have a smaller budget, for example, divergent salaries are understandable.

The second step is to broaden your data base. "The cornerstone of successful salary negotiation lies in knowing what your skills are worth on the job market," says Sherry Chastain, author of *Winning the Salary Game: Salary Negotiation for Women*.

Check available compensation surveys published by your trade associations, trade publications, or chamber of commerce. The American Management Association publishes general earnings data. Popular business magazines and management consulting or executive recruiting firms are other possible resources. Make use of the office grapevine to find out more about company-wide salaries, if possible. Inquire with friends and colleagues at conventions, trade shows, and seminars about salary levels for your comparable position at other companies.

Once you've gathered enough facts, there are several ways to approach your boss. Andrew J. DuBrin, author of *Winning at Office Politics*, suggests gentle confrontation. Don't put your boss on the defensive, because the error may not have been his or her doing," he explains. Try something like: "I have found out about a salary discrepancy that really concerns me."

From there, you might ask for a salary "adjustment" based on the facts you've collected.

When you bring up the salary discrepancy, be prepared for your boss's question: "How do you know what Jack or Karen makes?" Your best reply is that salaries are common knowledge through the grapevine. "Best not to finger anyone," warns Kennedy, even though it's illegal for an employer to penalize you for sharing salary information.

Your best bet for getting the raise you want, Chastain says, is to put together a proposal for meeting a need that isn't being addressed in your company. "Suggest that you'll take on this added responsibility in exchange for a specific dollar amount that will bring your salary in line with what you feel you should be earning."

If these strategies don't work, and you suspect discrimination on the basis of sex, race, or age, you may want to take legal action. Ellen Cassedy, coauthor of *9 to 5: The Working Woman's Guide to Office Survival,* points out that to do so you needn't retain an attorney, because the Equal Employment Opportunity Commission is designed to be used by groups or individuals without legal assistance.

"But," cautions DuBrin, "if you value your good relationship with the firm, use complaints to outside agencies as a last resort."

Whatever approach you choose, Barkley and Crystal counsel, "watch your attitude. This is not an adversarial situation." Instead, they believe, "it's an opportunity for you to demonstrate your negotiating competence and confidence. That skill may be important to the company in other ways."

Situation 3

You are told you're doing a fabulous job, that the company is delighted with your work. Instead of a raise, however, you're promoted from assistant manager to manager of your department. Your boss claims there's no money in the budget for a raise at this time. Though pleased with your new title, you feel shortchanged.

Based on your excellent record, how can you negotiate additional compensation, if not for now, then for later?

"In any situation, when your boss claims there is no money for a raise now, ask when the money will be available," advises Cassedy. "Then put it in writing and be sure to remind your boss at the appropriate time—and don't forget to ask that the raise be made retroactive."

Our experts agreed on this strategy but differed on the question of whether it's wise to check on your company's profitability or your department's budget to determine whether the claim of "no money" is justified.

"You should accept your boss's initial response that no money is in the budget," says Ilich, because if word gets out that you're checking, it will undermine the "bridge of goodwill" necessary to meaningful negotiations and weaken your position by conveying the message that you don't trust your boss's word.

But Kennedy counters, "The no-money plea is used in good times and bad to thwart raise requests from uninformed employees. It's up to you to stay on top of your company's financial health. The simplest way to do that is to read the company's annual report—assuming it has one."

It *is* in your interest to find out if the company is on its last legs, because if it is, chances of getting the raise you want are slim, and you may want to look elsewhere.

On the other hand, if your company has a good record overall, and is just weathering a bad spell, you may be in a better position to negotiate a raise than you would be in prosperous times. "Sometimes you can actually secure better financial footing when a company is in trouble and you successfully demonstrate how you are significantly contributing to a turnaround," says Kennedy. "The company just cannot afford to lose you."

McGlaughlin believes you clearly deserve a salary increase to match your increased responsibilities.

However, he continues, if a raise is impossible at this time, try negotiating these alternatives:

◆ A year-end bonus linked to agreed-upon performance objectives.

◆ Perks—club membership, a company car, tuition reimbursement, etc.

◆ A sizable stock option. Since a stock option does not involve a cash outlay for the company, it is a viable alternative if cash is really tight.

Don't underestimate the value of your promotion, even if unaccompanied by a deserved raise, agree the experts. "The promotion means more money to you, if not in your present company, then somewhere else," say Barkley and Crystal.

Whether it's perks, a promise of a healthy raise to come, or more money now, you should get some of what you want out of this situation. If you don't, it may be time to start quietly looking around for a new job from the greater vantage point of your new position.

Situation 4

You've been working for a year at the same salary. Over that period, your responsibilities have increased significantly, and you're handling them with ease and efficiency. You feel you deserve a raise, but the company has no set job performance and salary review procedure. You've hinted and joked that a raise might be in order—but the hints were ignored and the jokes enjoyed.

How do you clearly and unmistakably bring up the subject of a raise with your employer?

"Hints don't produce raises. Neither do jokes. Neither does wanting a raise, needing a raise, or deserving a raise," stresses Kravette.

Experts agree that allowing a year to pass without getting a raise—even if there is no formal salary review procedure—is a mistake.

Ask your immediate supervisor for a "performance review" to discuss how your work is progressing. Before the meeting, submit a written memo outlining your accomplishments over the past year, your added responsibilities, what you're doing to improve your skills, and any further responsibilities you'd like to take on. "This technique, in contrast to 'going in cold,' conditions your boss to give you a higher raise," says Chastain.

"This is also the time to feel out your potential," notes Thelma Kandel, author of *What Women Earn*. How far can you go in the company? Where does the boss see you in another year in terms of responsibility and salary?

Timing is important to success. "Approach your boss well before department budgets are set for the next year," advises DuBrin. And, adds Ilich, "select a time when your boss is in a positive mood."

When it's time to talk money, DuBrin believes, it's advisable to request the percent increase you think you deserve because the company probably does not have carefully developed guidelines of its own.

But Ilich disagrees: Have a definite amount in mind, but try to get the person granting the raise to set the amount. The reason is that if you name the figure, you've set the upper limit of your raise, which could be lower than what your boss had in mind. If your boss's figure is lower than what you feel is reasonable, you can negotiate up.

Always approach your immediate boss first when requesting a raise. That way, you avoid stepping on toes and can secure your boss as an ally. "But," adds McGlaughlin, "if your boss claims budgetary constraints, profit pressure, or lack of authority, you can legitimately ask for an interview with the next level of command."

Because Kennedy sees the situation as a struggle between

the company, which tries to get more out of you for the same money, and you, who must see that you're not exploited, she favors a more radical strategy: "Submit a new job description, title, and a new price tag for that job," she says. "Only then will you know if the company is really impressed with what you're doing or thinks it has found a sucker."

"When your boss says yes to a raise, thank him or her and get it in writing," suggests Cassedy. "If the answer is no, ask when you can discuss it again—and make sure you do!"

But Kandel points out that a negative response could mean it's time to look around for a company that can afford a decent wage policy.

Situation 5

You've been offered a job and considerably more money by another company. But you are happy in your current job (except for the salary) and would like to stay there and advance.

Can and should you use the job offer as leverage to secure a raise?

The short answer is yes, but *only* if you're prepared to take the other offer, should your employer show you the door.

Say Barkley and Crystal: "In this situation, as in all business negotiations, you have to be willing to move on if your needs aren't filled. You really can't negotiate if you don't view yourself as a free agent."

The job offer puts you in a "fairly easy negotiating position," according to Ilich.

But you may lose your advantage if you confront your boss with an ultimatum: "Give me a raise or else . . . I'll accept the new job."

As always, it's better to use tact. Indicate to your boss that you've received an offer for considerably more money, but that you prefer to stay where you are because you enjoy your work, like your boss, respect his or her leadership, etc.

As with Situation 4, outline your past contributions to the

company, and what you have in mind for the future. (Your boss may need to be reminded how valuable you are as an employee.) At the same time, suggest you'd like to arrive at some form of adequate salary increase.

You can expect one of three responses: a raise now; a plan whereby you can work toward a raise within a definite period of time; or an invitation to the door.

"In the first two instances," say Barkley and Crystal, "you'll have risen in the estimation of your boss for addressing the situation in a businesslike manner. In the last, it's clearly time to move on."

Kravette puts a slight twist on this strategy. "If you are happy in your present job except for the salary, you're *not* happy in your present job," he says. "But don't use the outside offer as leverage. *Do* use it as a focal point for communication with your boss."

The object of this communication is not to threaten your boss, but to find out what you need to do to get a raise. "Ask your boss for advice, mentioning that you'd rather stay, but you feel you owe it to yourself to consider the job offer as an opportunity to advance," Kravette suggests. "You'll find out exactly where you stand and then you'll know what to do next."

Two other participants in our survey also advised against using an outside job offer as leverage. "If you're concerned about money, but like your job, ask for a raise outright," suggests Kennedy. "Say you're not earning the going rate, but don't tell the company you've had a better offer."

DuBrin agrees and warns, "If you tell your boss you've received a better offer elsewhere, he or she may suspect you're disloyal and have been 'looking around.' If you wind up staying with the company, this could adversely affect your chances the next time you're considered for a promotion."

What should you do if any one of these strategies fails, and your request for a raise is turned down?

"You are not going to win every time you negotiate, but you will lose every time you don't," notes Chastain, who, along with Cassedy and Ilich, urge you to be "gently persistent" about your raise. Ask yourself and your boss if there are ways you could do your job better to strengthen your case for an increase. Then develop a new strategy and try again at your next review, or when a reasonable period of time has elapsed.

Above all, says Chastain, "don't take a failed raise strategy as a personal rejection. These discussions can be every bit as delicate as arms talks. Gentle and ongoing testing is the essence of negotiating success."

McGlaughlin and Kandel take a different point of view. If you know there's no more money in the immediate future, or you feel you're being treated unfairly, their advice is to initiate a formal job search, while still employed. "Companies always want to hire someone who already has a job, particularly at professional and managerial levels," points out McGlaughlin. "And remember," says Kandel, "you're frequently more attractive to another employer than to your own, who takes your good work for granted."

Kennedy suggests your response to a turndown should reflect an awareness of overall economic conditions: "The watchword of the 1980s is that you'll have to move to get more money because companies are examining the value of both the annual increase and the need to give more money. If inflation is at 4 percent, why give a 7 percent raise?"

If you're determined to stay, though, Kennedy supports other participants' recommendations to increase your productivity and thus your dollar value to your employer.

STRATEGIES FOR SMOOTH CAREER CHANGES

If the very last thing you want to be doing in five years is what you're doing now, you may be ripe for a career change.

Making that move will take a fair amount of courage and

plenty of planning. Especially important, most career changers will attest, is devising a realistic financial plan for your transition period, and beyond. Without it, your bid for a new career could plunge you and your family into a downward financial spiral that may be difficult—if not impossible—to recover from.

Among the questions you must address at the outset; Will your income take a serious dip initially? Will you lose company-paid health benefits that your family depends on? Will you have to sell off investments earmarked for your children's college expenses in order to fund a business of your own?

Questions like these shouldn't scare you off the career-change path. Instead, they'll allow you to make a realistic assessment of your prospects and face the inevitable ups and downs with greater confidence.

Assessing Your Assets

Before you calculate how much money you'll need, you have to figure out how much you have on hand. Write down the amount of your savings, investments, IRAs, pensions, property, and other tangible assets. Pay special attention to those that could help extend your credit: assets to be used as loan collateral, property you could mortgage.

Also include backup financial sources that you could sell or borrow against. Maybe you're a partner in a charter boat or own a share of a vacation home. Parents are another good source. Chances are they're looking at estate planning now, or would cash in a life insurance policy.

The John C. Crystal Center, the management planning firm, advises its career-change clients to determine the amount of cash they'll need to make the switch successfully. Says its president Nella Barkley, "To be prudent, the first rule of thumb is expect it to take considerably longer and cost considerably more than you think." She recommends these steps:

1. Keep a log of your expenditures for at least a month. Of course, the longer you do it, the more precise your esti-

mate will be. Save receipts for everything, and file them in an accordion folder. "You can't have an accurate picture unless you include everything," advises Barkley. "At the end of the period, add all the items and analyze them. You'll have an absolutely accurate picture of what you're spending, which will help you determine where *not* to spend."

2. While you're filing receipts, also keep a detailed calendar of daily activities. "At the end of the period," says Barkley, "look at the receipts and calendar together. You'll be able to tell immediately what items you can cut out. The little things you'll never miss—the bagel and coffee in the morning—can save you money in the long run."

3. Now draw three vertical lines separating a long sheet of paper into three columns. Label them "Minimum," "Comfortable," and "Optimum." These represent the three lifestyles you must visualize for your transition.

List all the expenses you'd have relating to that particular lifestyle in each column, being sure to include annual items (such as insurance premiums) as well as monthly expenses.

Work on the "Comfortable" column first. Then, if the expenses you tally wind up to be too high for what you think you'll be able to manage, start subtracting. If making a career change is that important to you, could you give up your club membership, take your children out of private school, forgo a vacation or two? Finally, when you've pared down all you can, you will end up with your "Minimum" survival level.

Now subtract any income you may have from sources other than work (such as investments) from the totals of these categories.

At this point you should have a fairly accurate idea of how much income you'll need to bring in. If the financial picture looks bleak, you may want to stay in your present job a while longer to build up a bigger reserve fund before you make a move.

Now take a look at the "Optimum column." Adding up the expenses required by your dream life-style can show you whether you want to go after the big bucks necessary to sustain it. Would the hours you'd need to put in to make $200,000 deprive you of time to enjoy the rewards? That's the sort of question that you alone can answer.

Whatever column you find most appealing, you'll probably discover that simply learning you could pare down your budget to make way for a career move can be a liberating experience.

Before You Leap

Whether you intend to work for someone else or strike out on your own, there are certain must-do's. For instance, have all necessary medical and dental work taken care of while you're still covered by your employer's policy. This should include checkups and physicals for family members as well.

Also, see if you can arrange with your employer for continued health care benefits. Just because you've had your annual physical doesn't mean you should take the chance and walk away uninsured. (See page 143 for information on your rights in this regard.) Even if you move to another employer, you may find a risky gap in your coverage.

Another possibility, although less common, is for your employer to keep you on the books and pay your health insurance in exchange for part-time work from you.

Also investigate your pension benefits. You may need additional capital and decide to cash it in. If you have only a year or two until you're fully vested, you may want to postpone your move so that you can get a larger payment down the line. But if you're more concerned that you have a retirement fund, see if you have the option of keeping the money in the plan even after you leave.

Of course, if you're starting your own business, consider a gradual switch, working at it part-time while keeping your current job. "If it's possible, go at it slowly," says Barkley. "This gives you more leverage, and you'll be more satisfied, knowing you can leave your present job when you want to."

Choosing a Career Counselor

If you're thinking about a job change, you may have considered going to a career counselor. Before you do, note that they are primarily *counselors* who concentrate on helping you discover your goals and strengths rather than on finding you a job.

Know, too, that there are counselors who will make promises they can't keep. "They tend to prey on people who are insecure or vulnerable, and aren't exercising their best judgment," says Paul Merry, an assistant attorney general of Massachusetts. His is one of thirteen states that have filed civil complaints against career counseling firms.

Warning Signs

To protect yourself, watch for these scam signals:

◆ The guarantee of a job—unless your career counselor plans to hire you.

◆ A large fee that must be paid *up front*, before any services have been delivered. (Fees are often based on your previous salary, and can range up to $10,000.)

◆ Promises of access to hidden, unpublished job markets, or contacts in high places. "You can't buy access into the old-boy network," says Merry, "even if these jobs really do exist."

◆ Claims that clients find jobs at higher salaries, or that the counselor won't represent people below a certain salary level, making his firm sound exclusive.

◆ Impressive, but meaningless, titles. The term "career counselor" isn't regulated; nor are "management consultant," "outplacement service," "executive search," or "career development." What various counselors (or charlatans) choose to call themselves won't tell you whether they're on the level.

To find a competent counselor, check out several—comparing prices, strategies, and methods. Ask for the following:

◆ References—and definitely call some. Former clients can tell you exactly what the counselor did for them. Check with the local Better Business Bureau or consumer protection agency to find out if any complaints have been lodged against your prospective counselor.

◆ A formal contract, stating exactly the services provided. "Pin them down in writing—so it doesn't come down to 'You said it,' 'No I didn't,' " says Erica Summers of the Federal Trade Commission.

◆ Certification. The National Board for Certified Counselors has been certifying career counselors who pass its requirements since mid-1985. Though certification is one positive indication, it's no guarantee.

◆ Background—education, length of time in practice, experience with people in your field.

Advice à la Carte

Some career counselors may package services that are available individually, and can be found for less money elsewhere, such as résumé drafting, interview training, and aptitude or psychological testing. Price these individual services before making a decision.

Also check out local community colleges and community outreach programs, which may offer free career counseling, recommends Frank Burtnett, formerly of the American Association for Counseling and Development. For the AACD's pamphlet, "Selecting a Professional Counselor—The Choice Is Yours," write AACD, Department U, P.O. Box 9888, Alexandria, Virginia, 22304. For a list of certified career counselors in your area, write the National Board of Certified Counselors, 5999 Stevenson Avenue, Alexandria, Virginia 22304.

Your Retirement Income ◆◆◆◆

TRYING to gauge, today, how much money you'll need to fund your retirement tomorrow is largely guesswork. Your estimate will fluctuate as your own living requirements change, and all figures will be scrambled by one large unknown—the average rate of inflation between now and the day you retire.

But one thing is certain: For a secure retirement you will need income from these sources: pension, Social Security, personal savings and investments, and perhaps even continued earnings from a part-time job or second career. "As a general statement, you need them all," says Paul Westbrook, benefits consultant and head of preretirement planning services at Buck Consultants in New York City. "Each is important to make up the whole."

Which element will supply the lion's share of retirement funds? The answer varies according to income level. For people sixty-five and older living in families with incomes of $25,000 or more, interest and dividends provide roughly 40 percent of personal income; Social Security, 21 percent; and pensions, 17 percent, according to a study by the Employee Benefits Research Institute. In families with incomes of $12,000 to $25,000, Social Security benefits are more important, providing 48 percent of personal income; interest and dividends, 22 percent; and pensions, 20 percent.

It should be noted that the $23,000-plus households derive an additional 20 percent of income from employment earnings, while the $10,000–$23,000 households derive only 8 percent of income from this source.

In the future, earnings from employment will play an increasingly important role in income for the sixty-five-plus population, Westbrook predicts. There are two reasons: (1) today's workers change jobs frequently, seldom staying with one company long enough to build up substantial pension benefits; and (2) though Social Security is said to be actuarially sound through the year 2040, Westbrook says benefits may begin to diminish after that.

As a result, unless Americans increase personal savings rates dramatically, many simply will not have enough money to retire on, and so will continue working long past the traditional, age-sixty-five retirement milepost. "That may not be the worst thing that could happen," Westbrook notes. "Now that mandatory retirement has been eliminated, people are beginning to realize that all work is not bad, and all play is not good. We're reshaping our ideas of what we need to do as human beings to be happy and challenged."

WHAT YOU WILL GET FOR YOUR SOCIAL SECURITY TAXES

While Social Security should not be considered the keystone of your retirement plan, the benefits it pays will provide an important *supplement* to other retirement income.

See Table 8 on page 182 for what you can expect to receive:

PENSIONS AND SUPPLEMENTARY RETIREMENT PLANS

Pensions come in two basic "flavors"—defined contribution and defined benefit. In a *defined contribution plan,* your employer sets a specific contribution amount—usually a set percentage of salary—and the proceeds are invested in a fund on your behalf. The proceeds at retirement are affected by the investment ability of the fund's manager.

TABLE 8 SOCIAL SECURITY BENEFITS		
For someone retiring at age 65 in	Your Estimated Annual Social Security Benefits (in 1987 dollars)	
	Average Earner (Earning $20,990 in 1990)[1]	Maximum Earner (Earning $49,200 in 1990)[2]
1990	$ 7,615	$10,316
1995	7,726	10,739
2000	8,283	11,954
2005	8,894	13,299
2010	9,555	14,704
2015	10,265	16,095
2020	11,027	17,355
2025	11,848	18,646
2030	12,727	20,029

[1] Now earning $18,000.
[2] Now earning $45,000.

Defined benefit plans, on the other hand, preset the amount of your benefits—your employer promises to pay you a specified (and guaranteed) pension based on your length of service and salary. Regardless of the company's profitability or investment performance, etc., the company's contribution each year must be adequate to fund that commitment to you at retirement.

Which is better for you? That depends on a number of factors such as age and health, employment history, and willingness to take risks for a potentially larger pension benefit. Defined benefit plans are guaranteed by the Pension Benefit

Guarantee Corporation, while defined contribution plans are not insured at all. With a good investment manager, however, the defined contribution plan, over time, may be worth more.

Another consideration: If you change employers, a defined contribution plan may allow you access to the cash value in your pension, even if your tenure with the company has been short, while defined benefit plans almost never do. (See "The Perils of Job-Hopping," page 186.)

Thrift plans. A thrift is any plan where your employer matches your contributions of after-tax income to a retirement savings account, often at a rate of 30 to 50 percent, but in some cases up to 100 percent. Your contributions to these accounts go untaxed until withdrawal. Add the power of compounding *and* the double-bang of the employer contribution and you begin to see how these accounts add up over time. And, since this is after-tax money you are contributing, some plans allow you to borrow from the account without tax penalty.

Salary "reduction" plans (also known as 401[k] plans or deferred arrangements, pay-conversion plans, or deferred-payment plans). Contributions to these plans are made in *pre-*tax dollars. This means the money you put away in a salary reduction plan does not show up in your paycheck, so your federally taxable income is reduced by the amount of your contribution. What's more, your contributions and the accrued earnings on them are tax-deferred until withdrawal. (The contribution tax-deferred *is* subject to Social Security tax, however, and in some states and cities you pay income tax on it as well.)

As an added incentive, many companies are matching employee contributions at rates from twenty cents to the dollar up to one-for-one match.

The 1986 tax law capped pretax contributions to the plan by the employee at $7,000 per year, or 15 percent of earned income, whichever is less. The $7,000 cap may be increased in years after 1987 by an inflation formula.

Profit-sharing plans. Basically these plans offer a means of sharing the proceeds of business with employees. As a pension, they have one major drawback: There is no way of anticipating the value of your final retirement benefit, since it is tied to the profitability of your employer.

Employee stock ownership plans. ESOPs are bonus or incentive programs whereby employees are typically given 5 to 10 percent of annual compensation in company stock. The management theory behind this plan is that employees who have a stake in the company work harder to see it succeed. As a retirement benefit, ESOPs can be shaky—stock prices go down as well as up and a bankruptcy will affect you as a stockholder as well as an employee.

Simplified employee pensions (SEP-IRAs). The SEP-IRA allows your employer to make an annual contribution equal to 15 percent of compensation or $30,000, whichever is less, to a retirement account established for all employees. Employees decide where the money is to be invested, and can exclude the amount contributed for a given year from their taxable income. Some employers allow voluntary employee contributions to a SEP-IRA as well, but these must not exceed $7,000 a year. You can take SEP-IRA holdings with you if you change jobs. If your new employer does not have this type of plan, just roll it over into an IRA. If you are self-employed, you may set up a SEP-IRA as a personal retirement savings plan. It is an alternative to the better-known Keogh.

Keogh plans. Though the Keogh is widely known as the retirement savings plan of the self-employed, the fact is that since 1982, Keoghs have increasingly grown to resemble corporate retirement plans. Today, one of the few major differences is that corporate plans have borrowing provisions and Keoghs do not.

Contributions to Keoghs are tax-deductible and tax-deferred until withdrawal, and you decide how to invest the funds.

Most self-employed people structure their Keoghs as *defined contribution* plans, selecting either a money-purchase Keogh or a profit-sharing Keogh. The former permits contributions of up to 25 percent of earned income or $30,000 each year. An additional stipulation: The designated contribution *must* be made on an annual basis. You are not permitted to skip a year.

Profit-sharing Keoghs permit contributions of up to 15 percent of compensation or $30,000, and you are allowed to designate the contribution amount—from 0 to 15 percent—each year.

You may set up both forms of defined-contribution Keoghs, if you wish, so long as you remain below the overall contribution limits of $30,000 a year or 25 percent of compensation (after Keogh contributions).

Keoghs may also be structured as *defined benefit* plans. This arrangement is best suited to people nearing retirement who want to make large contributions (larger than those permitted with defined contribution plans) over a short period of time. Contributions are figured according to a formula which determines the desired annual benefit, and the amount necessary to fund that benefit.

Rules are complex, so be certain to consult an accountant or actuary before setting up any type of Keogh plan.

The individual retirement account. The IRA is a voluntary, self-funded retirement planning vehicle for employed or self-employed individuals. The general rule is that you can invest up to $2,000 of your *earned* compensation annually as an individual, $2,250 for a combined spousal account. The funds may be invested in almost anything except collectibles. Your investment's earnings compound tax-free until withdrawal—usually at age 59½ or older. Under 1986 tax law revisions, contributions are fully deductible for workers who are (1) not covered by any other retirement plan, or (2) covered by another retirement plan, provided their adjusted gross income is less than $25,000 on an individual return, $40,000 on a joint return. The deduction will phase out for workers whose incomes fall between $25,000 and $35,000 ($40,000 and $50,000 for joint returns).

(For more on SEP-IRAs and Keoghs, see page 36.)

THE PERILS OF JOB-HOPPING

Job-hopping three times within a forty-year career span could cost you more than $100,000, in *defined benefit* pension payments when you retire—even if you're fully vested. That's according to a study by Dennis E. Logue, professor of management at Dartmouth College's Amos Tuck School of Business Administration. (Job-switching is also penalized by *defined contribution* plans, if you are required to wait before becoming eligible.)

So, if that new job offer is not attractive enough to offset the loss of thousands of dollars in pension benefits, prepare yourself to negotiate with your prospective employer for what you stand to lose.

(See Table 9, for the costs of job-hopping.)

TABLE 9 THE DOLLAR DAMAGE	
Job Status	Pension Benefits at Age 65
No job change	$206,000
1 job change after 20 years	118,000
3 job changes (1 every 10 years)	82,000
Source: Adopted by Peat Marwick from a chart that appeared in "Pension Plans at Risk," published by the National Center for Policy Analysis.	

Calculating your potential pension loss is a complicated affair. If you are thinking of changing companies, seek advice from the plan administrator of your present pension fund. (Request that your inquiry be kept confidential.)

To start you on the right track, here are some key questions to ask:

◆ What formula will be used to calculate my benefits?
◆ How long before I'm fully vested? (Thanks to the 1986 Tax Reform Act, you should be offered full rights to your retirement benefits after five years, down from ten years before the law passed.)
◆ What benefits can I expect if I stay with the company until retirement? What if I leave now?
◆ Will my pension be reduced by the amount of my Social Security benefits?

Other pertinent questions and information on your pension rights can be found in "A Guide to Understanding Your Pension Plan," published by the Pension Rights Center, 1701 K Street N.W., Suite 305, Washington, D.C. 20006, $3.50.

A FRESH LOOK AT IRAS

If sunning on a golden beach figures in your retirement reveries—to be financed by a bulging IRA account—the Internal Revenue Service has a splash of cold-water reality for you. The 1986 tax law not only made saving through individual retirement accounts less attractive for many Americans, it made withdrawing IRA funds more complicated. In essence, retirement nest eggs may get scrambled when taken out of the nest.

To understand the withdrawal wrinkles, it's helpful to consider how rules on IRA contributions have changed under tax reform. Under the old law, virtually anyone who worked (as well as nonworking spouses) could make tax-deductible IRA contributions. Accounts grew tax-deferred and withdrawals were taxed at the ordinary—and usually lower—tax rates that prevailed for retirees.

Under current law, the equation changes. Workers covered by an employer pension plan may or may not be able to make tax-deductible contributions to an IRA, depending on their adjusted gross income. Workers not covered by a pension plan still may make fully deductible contributions.

For those covered by a qualified plan. If you are single and your adjusted gross income is under $25,000 a year, you may make the full $2,000 deductible contribution. If you earn between $25,000 and $35,000, the Internal Revenue Service uses a contribution scale that slides downward from $2,000. And if you are single and earn over $35,000, your contributions to an IRA are nondeductible. For joint filers, the top income limit for any deductibility is $50,000.

From now on, people who continue to save through IRAs will wind up with two pools of savings: one arising from deductible contributions, and the newer one consisting of nondeductible contributions and their growth. For withdrawal purposes, you—the IRA owner—cannot decide the pool from which the funds are coming. The IRS does that for you.

The new rules tax your withdrawal on the basis of the nondeductible share of your total IRA assets. For example, assume you have $100,000 in your IRA: $80,000 in the deductible portion and $20,000 in nondeductible contributions. If you withdraw $10,000—regardless of the pool from which it is drawn—the IRS considers $2,000, or 20 percent of the withdrawal (the ratio of $20,000 to $100,000), to have come from the nondeductible IRA. The other $8,000 is considered to be from the deductible IRA and would face taxation.

To make recordkeeping easier, some accountants are advising their clients to start new IRA accounts for their nondeductible IRAs. Since the burden of recordkeeping falls on the IRA owner, not the bank, brokerage or mutual fund company acting as trustee, separate accounts eliminate many tax record headaches (but add to maintenance costs).

While other elements of IRAs have changed, the age rules for withdrawals haven't. IRA participants may withdraw funds without penalty after age 59½ and *must* begin withdrawals by April 1 of the year following the one in which they reach age 70½.

One positive aspect of the new law is the elimination of the 10 percent penalty for any early withdrawals that are structured as an annuity: Using life expectancy tables provided by the Internal Revenue Service, IRA investors may make penalty-free withdrawals *at any age* if the funds are taken out on a regular schedule, calculated to liquidate the account by the time of death.

However, withdrawals made in lump sums before age 59½ are still subject to the 10 percent penalty.

A new penalty applies to investors who withdraw too much from an IRA. When more than $112,500 is withdrawn from an IRA in one year, a 15 percent penalty is charged. If the overdraft is made by someone younger than 59½, the government drops the 10 percent early withdrawal penalty and assesses only the 15 percent penalty.

Yet another penalty is imposed on any funds that should have been withdrawn from an IRA by age 70½, but were not. In such cases, 50 percent of the sum that should have been withdrawn (based on IRS life expectancy tables) is subject to tax, even though the money is still in the IRA account. The sum will be taxed again, in full, when it is finally withdrawn.

Overall, the revised withdrawal rules, as well as the non-deductibility of contributions for many investors, make an IRA a less appealing investment than it once was. Still, most financial advisors contend that any device that permits tax-deferred growth is worthwhile, if the IRA investor plans to leave the account untouched for many years. What's more, keeping funds in an IRA while making withdrawals in the retirement years permits continued tax-deferred growth of the remaining principal. Such growth can add substantially to a retiree's wealth.

However, for individuals who may wish to tap their IRAs several years after making a contribution, tax-free municipal bonds may be a better choice, other advisors suggest, especially for those in higher tax brackets (28 and 33 percent in 1988). Tax-free munis may be sold any time before maturity with no penalty, although the price of municipal bonds, like all bonds, fluctuates with interest rates.

Another investment choice to consider might be single-premium universal life insurance, where the investment also grows tax-free, yet is available to be borrowed with no penalty.

"We're not giving our clients a blanket prescription *not* to invest in IRAs," said Larry Silver, a tax partner with the accounting firm Peat, Marwick and Mitchell Company in New York. "But I'm counseling against them for many of my clients.

"Withdrawals are complicated and expensive," he says, "because the investor cannot pull out money from the nondeductible IRA without triggering a tax payment on the deductible portion."

Securing Your Estate ♦ ♦ ♦ ♦

YOU may feel that there is no need to worry about federal estate taxes if you're familiar with the unlimited marital deduction, which allows you to leave any amount to your spouse, free of federal estate tax, and the exemption allowance, which from 1987 on permits you to pass a total of $600,000—also free of federal estate tax—to persons other than your spouse.

But if you figure in inflation and appreciation on your assets, there is a good chance that your estate is now over the $600,000 mark.

So you may be able to pass your estate to your spouse tax-free, but when he or she dies, your children (or other named heirs) will have to pay a hefty tax bill. If the estate is $800,000, for example ($200,000 over the $600,000 exemption limit), your children will have considerably less to inherit.

This money could have been passed on without a penny of federal estate tax owed, though, by using one or more of the following frequently overlooked estate-planning strategies:

FOUR WAYS TO CUT HEIRS' TAX BURDEN

1. Bypass Trusts

With bypass trusts, you and your spouse can pass up to $1.2 million in assets to your children or other beneficiaries, free of federal estate tax.

Take this example: A husband has a net worth of $1.2 million. In his will, he specifies that the first $600,000 of his estate be placed in a trust for the benefit of his wife during her lifetime, with their two children getting the assets after she dies. The remaining $600,000 is left directly to his wife (free of federal estate tax because of the unlimited marital deduction).

For as long as the wife survives the husband, she can receive all the income the trust earns and as much principal as she needs for health care, maintenance, support, and education. When she dies, the amount left in the trust is distributed between the two children, free of federal estate tax, because the trust is not considered part of the wife's estate. Any assets she owns in her own name *are* considered part of her estate. If that amount is under her exemption allowance of $600,000, the estate also passes tax-free to the children.

The underlying principle at work here is that by taking advantage of each spouse's exemption allowance, you can transfer combined assets over $600,000 and up to $1.2 million tax-free to your children or other beneficiaries.

But for bypass trusts to offer foolproof protection, both partners must have bypass provisions written in their wills, according to Martin A. Goldberg, an estate-planning attorney with the Connecticut-based law firm of Schatz, Schatz, Ribicoff and Kotkin. "If only one spouse has a will written with a bypass provision, and the spouse without one dies first and leaves all his or her assets directly to the survivor, you're back to square one—that is, you have only the surviving spouse's exemption allowance to shelter the combined assets."

2. Optional Bypass Trusts

While bypass trusts and optional bypass trusts are identical in principle (they're both tax-saving tactics that utilize each partner's exemption limit), they're created in different ways.

A bypass trust is automatically established upon the death of the first spouse. An optional bypass trust, on the other hand, comes into being only if the surviving spouse deems it necessary or desirable for tax purposes.

With the optional bypass trust, each spouse leaves his or

her estate outright to the surviving spouse. The survivor is, however, given the right to "disclaim" some or all of the property in the will, usually up to $600,000. This disclaimed property would then pass into a trust that would eventually be inherited by, say, the children, but could be used by the surviving spouse for his or her benefit until death.

If the combined assets of you and your spouse are below $600,000 now, but could appreciate by the time you or your surviving spouse dies, optional bypass trusts are an excellent way to safeguard your combined assets from potential taxes, according to Arnold D. Kahn, an attorney who specializes in wills, trusts, and probate, and author of *Family Security Through Estate Planning*.

On the other hand, if your assets will clearly need to be tax-sheltered, an outright bypass trust may serve your needs better. Says Kahn; "It spares your husband or wife from having to become involved in detailed legal discussions or having to make financial decisions right after your death."

3. Irrevocable Life Insurance Trusts

Life insurance proceeds are not subject to any federal estate tax if the beneficiary of the policy is your spouse (a result of the unlimited marital deduction again). But if your beneficiary isn't your spouse and the proceeds would hike your estate to over $600,000, or if the proceeds from the life insurance policy on which your spouse *is* the beneficiary push his or her estate over that $600,000 tax exemption allowance, then either your estate or your spouse's (upon his or her death) will have to pay federal estate tax.

The way around that? Rather than owning the policy yourself or giving it to your spouse, you put the policy into an irrevocable life insurance trust. Upon your death, the policy adds no tax to your estate, because you don't own it: The trust does. The proceeds are then paid into the trust. Your spouse gets the benefits of income, and principal as needed, for his or her life. Then, upon his or her death, the remainder of the proceeds flow down to your beneficiaries, totally free of federal estate tax.

Keep in mind that if you transfer an existing insurance policy to an irrevocable trust within three years of death, the insurance will be taxed as part of your estate, according to Goldberg. "However, if you transfer cash to the trust to buy a new policy, the proceeds are sheltered immediately."

4. Generation-Skipping Trusts

When the family fortune is over $1.2 million at death, you can't bypass taxes entirely, but you can reduce the tax bill with generation-skipping trusts.

Let's say, for example, that you have three children and several grandchildren. If you leave your estate to your children without placing it in a trust, then it may be taxed when you die and again when they die. In other words, your property would have been taxed twice before the grandchildren inherit it.

With a generation-skipping trust, you can eliminate the tax at your children's level. You simply will your estate into three separate trusts, one for each of your children, with ultimate distribution to go to your grandchildren. Your children's trusts continue for life, with each receiving trust income and principal payments as needed. Upon each of your children's deaths, the trusts would not be taxed, under the condition that the total amount you passed on to your children in trust *at your death* did not exceed $1 million.

The theory behind generation-skipping trusts is clear-cut. However, the laws on them are especially complex, so it's important for you to retain a lawyer who's well versed in this branch of tax law.

Note: "Get an expert's advice" is the across-the-board rule for using any of these estate-planning strategies. Only with the help of a lawyer or tax advisor will you be able to see if and how these tools could reduce your overall tax bill.

TRANSFERRING ASSETS FROM ONE GENERATION TO ANOTHER

The enormous pleasure derived from giving to those you love is perhaps the best reason for transferring assets from one generation to another. A more complex reason can be to save on overall tax bills. Assets can be money or gifts such as real estate, stocks and bonds, insurance policies, and interests in small businesses.

Transferring money or property from high-bracket family members to family members with less income and fewer assets can be complicated and requires careful planning and professional advice. A strategy to save estate taxes can backfire by increasing income taxes, creating a need to pay a gift tax, or making it harder for an older family member to get Medicaid benefits.

A basic goal of family tax planning is to protect every family member from possessing a taxable estate. To accomplish that, assets are often given away or left largely to the surviving spouse. Another aim is to avoid paying taxes on any increase in the value of assets, such as the appreciation of a family home or of stocks purchased years before.

Through 1986 it was important to find ways to get income taxed as capital gains, rather than at the higher rate for ordinary income. But, starting in 1987, the special treatment for capital gains was reduced and in 1988 eliminated. Overall tax rates were lowered.

Giving Programs

A person with a taxable estate (more than $600,000, beginning in 1987, excluding amounts left to the spouse or to charity) can reduce it by giving away assets. You can give any number of people up to $10,000 a year each, without incurring a gift tax. If the giver's spouse agrees to join in the gift (by signing a federal gift-tax return; he or she doesn't have to provide any

❖ ———————————————————————— **195**

of the gift), the couple can give up to $20,000 a year to any one person. A hint: If family members need a lot of funds (say, to buy a house), give $10,000 (or $20,000, with your spouse's consent) in December, and make another gift in January. Of course, a giving program also can be used to transfer stock or real estate.

Real Estate

By transferring income-producing real estate (an apartment building or business property), you give another family member not only a source of income, but also tax deductions for repairs and depreciation. In addition, you remove a sizable asset from your own estate, which could bring it under the taxable level.

If you transfer real estate to parents or other older relatives, they get both the valuable asset and the security of knowing they have a home for life, without fear of rent increases or eviction. If an older family member transfers real estate to members of a younger generation who are in a higher tax bracket, younger members get cash flow from the rent they receive, plus the benefit of tax deductions, in addition to the property. In fact, if an agreement is properly structured, the person who makes the transfer can continue to use the real estate that was transferred, while the person in the higher tax bracket continues to get the tax benefits.

A few cautions are in order. First, if real estate is transferred to minors, they'll need a guardian or custodian under the Uniform Gifts to Minors Act. If no guardian is named, and the property is to be mortgaged, sold, maybe even improved, a lengthy and expensive court proceeding will be required to name one. And then the new appointed guardian may have to go to court to get consent for these actions.

Second, to save taxes, any transfer within a family must be a real transfer. In case of an IRS audit, it's helpful to be able to prove that the transfer was made for nontax business purposes: The property was transferred to a relative who can manage it full-time, for example. There must be a valid deed, recorded in the same way as transactions between strangers. It may be all right for the person transferring to continue to manage the property—and even to get management fees—if the deal meets all the legal requirements.

Private Annuities

In a private annuity, one person transfers property to another. The person receiving the property agrees to pay the donor a certain amount every month throughout the donor's lifetime. Tax consequences are better if payments are *not* secured by collateral.

A private annuity serves to get the asset out of a taxable estate, and to provide high monthly returns in its place. Only a portion of each annuity payment is taxable income; the rest is considered a return of part of the purchase price, and this is not taxable. There's no gift tax, because there's no gift— the purchaser pays for the property.

Private annuities can be used to shift the ownership of valuable property that the current owners don't need to live on. Owners of small businesses can use private annuities to transfer stock ownership to the next generation, while collecting an additional source of retirement income.

Life Insurance

While giving a life insurance policy doesn't seem all that festive, it can be a way to make a large gift at a low cost. The strategy is to convert an existing policy to reduced "paid-up insurance" and assign it to whomever your beneficiary would be. Or you could buy a single-premium policy and make the same assignment.

You lose the right to borrow against the policy or change the beneficiary after giving it away. But you can continue making the premium payments. The new policy owner can now borrow against the cash value (which could be an excellent source of college funds for a child). If your purpose is to reduce the size of your estate, be aware that insurance gifts made within three years of death are added back into the estate.

SECURING THE FUTURE OF A DISABLED CHILD

At the top of the list of painful problems confronting parents of handicapped and disabled children is planning for the day when they won't be there to care for their sons and daughters.

No one enjoys estate planning, and most of us indulge the tendency to postpone this chore. Indeed, a shocking 70 percent of Americans die without a will! But it's critically important for parents to overcome this instinct and safeguard their children's future. Without a carefully drawn plan, sudden death or injury to the parents can have unforeseen—and unhappy—results. Well-meaning friends and family who have to make hasty arrangements may mishandle important legal and personal issues. *Or—and this is the deepest fear that haunts every parent of a disabled child—no one will be available to look after the child's interests according to the parents' wishes.*

Many factors contribute to the inertia parents so often display, estate planners report. Often, parents fail to realize that they ought to make special provisions for their child; others believe that only the wealthy have to worry about estate planning (and can afford to pay for it); many expect that the government will provide for their child after they're gone. And, of course, parents may simply be overwhelmed by the need to provide solutions for immediate problems.

But at a time when government benefits are under review and attack, parents shouldn't rely on them to meet the child's lifetime needs. Social and economic changes suggest that eventually the alternatives available to disabled children may change as well. Parents can and should see to it that they provide for continuity of support for their child's entire lifetime by designating someone to look after the child's interests and by setting up financial mechanisms to provide for future needs.

Where to get help. Figuring out where to start and who to turn to for professional help can be a daunting prospect. Many well-respected estate planners lack experience in making arrangements for clients with handicapped children. But detailed, current knowledge of state and federal regulations is crucial to setting up a successful plan that can withstand any court challenges, should they occur.

To help parents find appropriate advisors, local organizations such as the Association of Retarded Citizens (ARC), local chapters of United Cerebral Palsy, and other developmental disability organizations frequently can provide recommendations and guidelines. (See source list, page 203.)

"Seek out someone who's done this before," advises B. John Ready III, a Kansas City lawyer who, with Chris Hinken of Christopher T. Hinken & Associates, has prepared many such plans.

But before the first meeting with a lawyer can take place, parents will want to review their own goals and circumstances.

Getting organized is crucial, notes Hinken. Essentially, he says, there are *four key steps.*

1. A thorough evaluation of the child. "You can't draw up any estate plan until you know at exactly what level the child will function," Hinken says. "The plan for a child who is trainable, who will be educated and eventually self-sufficient, will be completely different than one for a child who will always be dependent on others."

2. Define the objectives for the child's care. What kind of situation and environment do you want to create for your child?

Possibilities include appointing a guardian, a conservator, or designating a relative to take care of the child. Alternatives include state institutions and halfway or residential houses, whether publicly supported or privately funded.

At this point, Hinken and others note, if the child will spend his or her life in a state institution, relatively little planning will be needed or, indeed, be desirable.

Once parents figure out where—and how—they want their child to live, they can begin to:

3. Consider what financial resources to make available and how to fund the plans. A number of possibilities exist. Chief among them is life insurance, which will actually create an estate for the child's use. But other possibilities include Supplemental Security Income (SSI), Social Security benefits, annuities, stocks and bonds, and gifts, to be used alone or in some carefully arranged combination.

Each method requires careful thought and explanation because of the complex technical issues involved in meeting parents' objectives. In addition to providing the funds, parents will need to consider who will be looking after the finances, and how, if at all, funds will be replenished.

All the preparation culminates in the final and most complicated step:

4. Set up a method to transfer the money to the child. How the funds are doled out, and by whom, makes all the difference in the world. Precise planning is needed to preserve the child's eligibility for government benefits, if parents want them.

Parents will also want to select people to protect their child's various interests. "Parents can't even find a baby-sitter for their handicapped child, let alone someone to take care of the child after they die," Hinken says. "And this choice is absolutely crucial to the success of any plan."

In fact, selection of guardians is so complicated that only an attorney can explain the options and responsibilities. Once a child reaches the age of maturity, guardianship laws and related considerations will help shape the outcome of the plan.

Every estate planner and counselor agrees: Parents should name several persons, in succession, in their wills to serve as guardians. If the first person changes his or her mind or for some other reason can't serve, the next person, or the third, can fill that obligation.

Early in the process, every parent will realize the importance of having a will. If a parent with a disabled child dies without leaving one, his or her property will be distributed according to state laws of intestacy, which will not take into account the parents' wishes or a child's disabilities.

Worse—inheriting property outright can work *against* a disabled child. On the one hand, the heir may not be able to cope with the money or property. On the other, if the child lives in a state-sponsored institution, the state may charge him or her for care—and those bills, in most cases, will devour the inheritance.

Since most states do not require parents to provide support for their children after their own deaths, some parents may elect to disinherit disabled children, even though this step may cause great emotional pain. It will be the sensible choice for some, but the decision should be based on expert legal advice.

"But parents don't *have* to disinherit a child," says Elaine Petersen, formerly a future-planning specialist with Oregon's ARC. "They can leave things as they want them to be for their child, if they establish a testamentary trust in their will."

Also, she and other planners suggest that parents prepare a written statement (a letter of intent), in addition to the will, that spells out their wishes and expectations and defines the duties they want the guardian to fulfill. For instance, this document may specify where the parents want the child to live, mention visiting arrangements with other relatives, and provide for participation in religious services.

Depending on family circumstances, most lawyers will recommend that plans include a trust for the benefit of the disabled offspring. They are unanimous in asserting that this trust must be drafted with great precision to ensure that it successfully meets its objectives and prevents the government from tapping assets to pay for state-sponsored care. Proper wording protects the trust's assets by making it clear that the assets are not owned by the beneficiary. And assets are crucial in determining eligibility for programs such as SSI.

One example of a trust document is the Craven Trust, named for a family in Washington State. "The trust was created with the idea of preserving eligibility for such programs as Supplemental Security Income," says Tom O'Brien of the Foundation for the Handicapped in Seattle. "Anyone who has an estate that they want to pass over for a handicapped son or daughter is well advised to protect the trust from invasion by the government."

Because of widely varying state laws, the trust document that works in one state may be disallowed in another. "Parents must use trusts with caution," notes Petersen. "There's never been a test case in Oregon, for example, but that doesn't mean one won't come up."

Hinken, too, expects eventual court challenges, but he stresses that a challenge doesn't mean the plan won't work.

Many organizations are preparing sample trusts for use by parents of handicapped children. The South Dakota Guardianship Program was told that the discretionary trust it developed could allow the beneficiary to have available the trust resource and still be eligible for federal entitlements. Of course, income from the trust to the handicapped person would have to be considered carefully so as not to jeopardize benefits. Accordingly, says Robert J. Kean, an attorney with the South Dakota Advocacy Project, this means that government benefits can't be denied or removed from beneficiaries of this particular trust on the basis of the resource it provides. "Parents can now provide funds to pay for a long list of items that Medicaid, for instance, doesn't cover," he says. "Items such as cosmetic surgery, and certain kinds of dental work."

That recent development underscores the importance of periodic review of all these arrangements and documents. "If there are legal or regulatory changes and older documents aren't brought up-to-date," says Kean, "the benefits might be put in jeopardy. Parents thought they were doing one thing, but the results could be very different."

Unless a family is wealthy, the most likely mechanism to guarantee funds will be life insurance. It can be especially helpful to those with disabled children, even if they have sizable assets. "If the proceeds are paid to a named beneficiary," Hinken says, "they pass outside of probate and immediately create the funds."

Perhaps even more important, if the proceeds of the policy are used to fund an irrevocable trust set up for the child's support, and the trustee is the named beneficiary, most states will not consider the child the owner. Consequently that insurance benefit won't threaten the child's eligibility for government benefits.

The amount of life insurance necessary will depend on the plans made to spend it and how much the family can currently afford to set aside.

Hinken suggests that parents normally look at a minimum of $100,000 in life insurance to fund a trust. And he advises a team approach with a lawyer to guarantee that the financial plans are successfully integrated with the legal requirements.

Reflecting on what he considers the primary benefit of this intensive planning, Hinken says, "The best gift parents can leave their other children is a workable plan so they won't be financially responsible for their handicapped brother or sister, even if parents have to leave their entire estate to that one child."

Sources

Parents and estate planners who want to get detailed advice can turn to the following sources:

◆ Local chapters of groups such as the Association of Retarded Citizens, United Cerebral Palsy, and National Epilepsy League have information on hand.

◆ Officials at state departments of social services will know of any special estate-planning programs.

◆ The local bar association can provide referrals to estate planners. Stress the need for a lawyer with special expertise in planning for and working with the disabled.

◆ The Foundation for the Handicapped in Washington State makes available copies of the Craven Trust. This model document, while tailored to Washington law, provides useful background and advice for both parents and lawyers. The booklet includes a checklist of information that parents should attach to their wills and a memo to lawyers explaining the reasons for the language used in the trust document, including an example of a case that didn't hold up in court because it was worded incorrectly. For a copy send $2.00 to the Foundation for the Handicapped, 1550 West Armory Way, Suite 205, Seattle, Washington 98119.

◆ The Guardianship, Advocacy, and Protective Services (GAPS) program of the Association for Retarded Citizens of Oregon has prepared two essential booklets for parents and estate planners. Each is clearly written, outlines the steps to take, and notes the myriad details to consider.

Although the booklets were written for residents of Oregon, many principles cross state lines; they are available by writing to 1745 State Street, N.E., Salem, Oregon 97301 (503)581-2726.

A Future Planning Guide for Parents of Developmentally Disabled Persons is free to Oregon parents; families outside the state should send a check for $3.50 with their letter.

Mark Russell, an Illinois attorney with a mentally handicapped brother, has written *Alternatives: Family Guide to Legal and Financial Planning for the Disabled,* to guide parents about to embark on estate planning. The paperback is available for $11.95, from ARC/Illinois, 700 South Federal, Suite 123, Chicago, Illinois 60605 (312) 922-6932).

Safeguarding Your Money ◆◆◆◆

YOU'RE only as secure as the institutions you entrust with your money—a reality which, in today's uncertain financial times, has left many depositors and investors plenty nervous.

What are the chances that your life savings could be diminished because of the default of your bank, brokerage firm, the insurance company managing your annuity, or the issuer of a municipal bond you've invested in?

Not high—but not out of the question.

Before entrusting your money to any institution, it's important to understand the risks, and the guarantees available to you, so you can judge how safe your money really is. The following pages compare how well your money is protected in banks, brokerage firms, municipal bonds, and annuities.

Banks

Banks, savings and loans, and credit unions have long touted themselves as safe storehouses of the nation's money. You're justified, however, if you raise a skeptical eyebrow at this claim, for events in the last few years have left many financial institutions in a weakened condition.

More depositor institutions have been liquidated or merged with stronger counterparts in the last three years than at any time since the Great Depression. In a few instances, depositors actually lost money.

Despite the much publicized collapses of banks such as Penn Square and Continental Illinois, and Bank of America's financial woes, most depositors remain unconcerned about the safety of their money. Of the nation's roughly 15,550 commercial and mutual savings banks, all but about 760 are insured by the Federal Deposit Insurance Corporation (FDIC). The Federal Savings and Loan Insurance Corporation (FSLIC) performs a similar role for about 3,200 S and L's and savings banks across the country; another several hundred S and L's fall under the protection of state insurance funds and private insurers; leaving just 61 S and L's in 1984 with no form of depositor insurance at all. (No current figures on uninsured S and L's are available.)

(Note: Be particularly wary if your deposits are *not* federally insured. As recent S and L failures in Ohio and Maryland have illustrated, private and state insurance funds cannot always make good on depositors' claims.)

Credit unions are usually insured, too. The National Credit Union Administration (NCUA) is the largest insurer, responsible for 96 to 98 percent of all credit unions. (The 2 to 4 percent not under NCUA's jurisdiction must adhere to state regulations, though they may not be insured.)

Thus it's unlikely that your deposits—whether in a bank, S and L, or credit union—are not covered by some sort of insurance program.

You can tell which government agency insures your money simply by looking for a membership seal the next time you visit your branch. These identification stickers must be displayed prominently and can usually be found at entrances and teller windows, as well as on any official brochures or advertising.

Insurance protection offered by the FDIC, FSLIC, and NCUA is free to depositors and is remarkably similar in most other ways. The federal government backs all three agencies, should their reserves prove insufficient.

Although most people assume their *accounts* are insured, this is, in fact, a misconception of some importance. *Accounts are not insured; depositors are.* Whatever type of conventional account(s) you use—checking, savings, money market, or certificate of deposit—your money is insured to an aggregate of $100,000. Thus, if you hold three accounts with deposits totaling $125,000, you are insured only up to $100,000, including principal and interest.

As a joint-account holder you are further constrained by the rule that depositors with interests in more than one jointly owned account are insured to a total of $100,000 on their interests in all of these accounts.

You may, however, qualify for greater coverage if your accounts are maintained in different rights or capacities. For instance if you are self-employed, your business and personal accounts would be separately insured.

All this does not mean that if your deposits surpass the $100,000 mark, they will have to go uninsured! On the contrary: When you reach $100,000 you can simply open an account at another insured bank, S and L, or credit union to house the excess. If you prefer keeping your banking business under one roof, there are other options. The following accounts have the advantage of being insured separately from any other accounts at the same institution by the FDIC, FSLIC, and NCUA:

IRA or Keogh accounts. The FDIC protects IRA and Keogh plans kept in demand deposit accounts to a maximum of $100,000. At the same time, funds kept in time deposit accounts are separately insured for up to another $100,000. The FSLIC makes no such distinction between types of accounts used to store IRA and Keogh monies. IRA accounts are insured separately from Keogh accounts, each to the $100,000 limit. The NCUA insures both types of accounts together, up to a total of $100,000.

Testamentary accounts. These accounts are also called revocable trust accounts. Each beneficiary who is a spouse, child, or grandchild of the owner is insured separately up to a total of $100,000.

Irrevocable trusts. The trust interest of a beneficiary in these accounts is insured up to $100,000 separately from the individual accounts of the trustee.

In the event that a bank, savings and loan, or credit union fails, and the regulators must step in to liquidate assets, insured depositors can expect to be fully paid off within one week to ten days of the closing. Depositors enjoy no such speed on amounts in excess of insurance maximums; while they may receive all or a portion of the money not insured soon after the institution's closure, there is no guarantee that this will happen. Those depositors with uninsured funds have a pro rata stake in the proceeds along with other general creditors, and the liquidation process usually drags on indefinitely.

Renee Kaplan, a banking examiner who reviews banks for the state of California, recommends depositors pay close attention to an institution's overall profit performance, interest expense in relation to interest income, and nonperforming loans as percentage of the loan portfolio (all this information can be found in your bank's annual report). Your suspicions should be aroused if the institution relies on deposits placed by professional money managers for higher-than-average interest rates or if it offers higher rates than other area institutions—these policies could signal serious cash flow problems. Another important danger sign is an abnormally high percentage of loan losses or delinquencies when compared to other financial institutions.

Specific questions you may have about insurance coverage on your accounts or about financial reports available to help you evaluate your financial institution can be obtained by writing or calling the pertinent regulatory agency's public information office. The FDIC has a toll-free consumer hotline—(800) 424-4334; you can write for information at 550 Seventeenth Street, N.W., Washington, D.C. 20429. The FSLIC's main information number is (202) 377-6934. Its headquarters address is 1700 G Street, N.W., Washington, D.C. 20552. The NCUA can be reached at (202) 357-1050 or 1776 G Street, N.W., Washington, D.C. 20456. You may also want to check with your bank, savings and loan, or credit union for the number and address of a regional office closer to you or for information about any other agency that insures your money.

❖

Brokerage Firms

How much can you trust your brokerage firm to safeguard your money, especially if the firm itself runs into financial difficulty? The 1970 Securities Investor Protection Act shields investors through an agency known as the Securities Investor Protection Corporation.

SIPC is a nonprofit membership corporation that promotes confidence in domestic securities markets by protecting owners of registered securities. It is not a government agency or a regulatory authority; it is funded by member broker-dealers.

If a member fails, SIPC appoints a trustee to liquidate the firm and represent the firm's customers. In cases involving smaller firms, SIPC may cover the losses out of its funds directly. The trustee may also elect to transfer all customer accounts to another broker in order to minimize disruption to customers' trading.

If a transfer of accounts is not possible, and the liquidating firm has available the total amount of securities which it held for customers, holdings registered in customers' names are sent to them. If the firm does not have the securities on hand to meet all customer claims, customers will receive securities on a pro rata basis, with cash disbursements made for the remaining securities.

In the event a firm in liquidation does not have securities or sufficient funds to settle all claims, the remaining claims of each account held by a customer will be settled by SIPC, up to a maximum of $500,000, including $100,000 cash. SIPC then assumes the debts of the customers and becomes the principal debtor in subsequent bankruptcy proceedings against the firm.

There are some exceptions to the $500,000 coverage rule, however. Only cash and securities (stocks, bonds, CDs, and notes) are protected. No coverage is offered for unregistered investment contracts such as gold, silver, commodities investments, or options. And cash is protected only so long as the money is under deposit or left in a securities account for the purpose of a pending purchase.

The term *security* also includes publicly registered investment contracts and certificates of participation in any profit-sharing agreements and oil, gas, or mineral leases and royalties. Investors' rights and warrants to buy, sell, or subscribe to any of the above-mentioned types of securities are also protected.

Although shares in a money-market mutual fund are often thought of as cash by investors, they are in fact securities and therefore covered under the $500,000 SIPC rules. If you frequently carry uninvested credit cash balances on your account, inquire about setting up an automatic sweep feature. Having your broker regularly move inactive cash balances into a money market fund means your money will always be covered.

Some brokerage firms carry insurance coverage on accounts in excess of $500,000. The firm will usually tell its "big" customers about excess coverage and if the firm does not, individuals should ask what their coverage limit is.

The $500,000 coverage limit applies to accounts held by individuals, but there are ways to extend your coverage. You may have more than one covered account, but they must be held in separate capacities—jointly with a spouse, trustee for a child, business account, etc. Under the SIPC rules, all accounts under one name would be limited to a total coverage of $500,000, so you may wish to broaden your coverage by spreading your accounts either in different capacities or at several different firms.

Coverage limitations also apply to claims placed by certain groups of investors and customers, primarily those with interests in the firm itself. SIPC will not recognize claims by a customer who is also a general partner, officer, or director of the firm; owns 5 percent or more of any class of equitable security in the firm; is a limited partner with a 5 percent or greater participation in the net assets or profits of the firm; or has controlling interest in the management or policy decisions of the firm. SIPC covers losses incurred only by the failure of the firm—*not* those sustained through bad investments or securities transactions.

If, in addition to insurance coverage, investors wish to examine the financial condition of their brokerage firm, information is available. The Securities and Exchange Commission suggests two sources, the SEC "one file" and "two file." The one file contains the firm's original application, listing officers, areas of business, and all pertinent information on its registration as a broker-dealer in securities. The two file contains the firm's annual and semiannual financial statements and notes, including any public litigation against the firm. You can request these reports from the SEC or your broker. For general information about brokerage firms or about insurance coverage of broker dealers and investor accounts, contact the Office of Consumer Affairs and Information Services, Securities and Exchange Commission, Washington, D.C. 20549.

Municipal Bonds

The Washington Public Power Supply (known by the acronym WHOOPS) debacle caused some investors to be squeamish about municipal bond investments. "How can you know how safe bonds are," they reflected, "when even reputable brokers were backing WHOOPS bonds?" A good question.

There are three risk considerations in selecting municipal bonds as an investment. Increases in interest rates can wreak havoc with the resale value of your bonds, for bond prices move down as rates go up—and vice versa. Second, financial difficulties for the issuer can mean bad news for the investor. And third, inflation can erode the value of long-term bond investments.

Municipal bonds are the debt obligations issued by states, towns, and other municipal bodies to raise funds. And, like all other borrowers, some municipalities have better borrowing records than others.

While over time the chances of an issuer defaulting have proved minimal, you can improve your odds on a safe investment by looking at the rating on a municipal bond. Based on the credit record of the issuer in previous bond issues, the bond's security or repayment pledge, the financial condition of the municipal borrower, and whether the issue carries insurance, ratings can lead you to the highest-quality investments. Ratings are published by several services, but the two major ones are Moody's Investment Service and Standard & Poor's.

For premium quality and security, the triple- and double-A bonds are best, but these ratings are not meant as guarantees. If you want a guarantee, look for a bond issue that bears insurance on the principal and interest.

You pay a premium for this no-risk protection, however: The yield is usually slightly less than on an uninsured bond.

Choosing the safest and most appropriate municipal bond for your investment goals and risk tolerance also requires good information. You should always read the "Offering Circular" on an issue carefully. Check the repayment pledge agreement on principal and interest, and know the credit record of the issuer or backer. In the resale or secondary market, this information can be difficult to track down, but is well worth asking your broker for.

As individual investors, you can "get into bonds" for $5,000 or more, since municipal bonds are usually offered in $5,000 increments. Discount or zero-coupons can be had for very low prices, and unit trust or bond mutual fund investments (described below) can be as low as $1,000.

Safety for investors goes beyond ratings, insurance, and price when you consider a bond purchase, however. It includes being able to sell your bonds with ease should a need for liquidity arise. In selecting a bond for investment, ask your broker how marketable your choice will be.

Variety and diversification are also a safety net.

One way to achieve diversification is to invest in a unit trust or bond mutual fund rather than buying individual bonds yourself. Unit trusts and bond funds offer all the best features of bonds—plus professional management, diversification, and convenience.

There are two principal differences between these accounts, however. Unit trusts are "closed-end," meaning that bonds purchased for the trust's portfolio remain in it until maturity or until other circumstances affect the viability of the bond. Most bond funds are "open-end," that is, they constantly receive more money from investors and their investments change as their managers continue to buy and sell issues. (Some bond funds are closed-end without an infusion of new monies. But unlike unit trusts, their managers do switch issues by selling some bonds and buying others with the proceeds of the sales.) The other difference is that unit trusts usually charge 3½ to 5 percent of the price of an offering, while bond funds charge an annual management fee (some charge a sales commission known as a "load"). (Closed-end bond funds are bought and sold through stockbrokers, like individual issues.)

TYPES OF MUNICIPAL BONDS

General obligation bonds are backed by the issuer on a pledge of full faith and credit for payment of principal plus interest. Many municipal bonds of this type are also secured by property taxes and other tax resources.

Revenue bonds are secured by income earned from a revenue-producing municipal enterprise, such as toll roads, water or power supply systems, or public transportation.

Authority or agency bonds are backed by the right or power of a municipality to levy fees and charges for services.

Limited and special tax bonds are payable from the proceeds of a specified tax or charge, such as an assessment or fuel tax.

Lease-secured bonds are backed by the pledge of a party other than the issuer, or borrower, frequently a bank or other institution whose credit record is superior to that of the issuer. A similar arrangement to watch for is the municipal bond secured by a bank-issued letter of credit.

These are the most common offerings, but there are others. Check with your broker for details on the financing behind any bond investment.

Annuities

Annuity: The very word evokes an image of safety and dependability. Indeed, the key attraction of this insurance product is the predictable, secure nature of the investment. Investors buy annuities in order to watch their principal grow, unhampered by taxes until they start to withdraw the money.

At least that's how it used to be. Well-publicized difficulties encountered by the Baldwin-United Company and the Charter Corporation, both major sellers of annuities, dented and rechanneled the market. In both cases, the parent companies went bankrupt, leaving those who held annuities bought from the insurance subsidiaries anxious and confused about the eventual payout of their investments. One aftershock of those tremors: Investors turned away from newer, less-tested companies to the old-line insurance companies.

Other developments have also diminished the appeal of annuities: volatile interest rates, periodic changes in the tax code, and the proliferation of investments for IRAs, Keogh plans, and other retirement nest eggs.

Despite some slippage, however, annuities remain very big business, and are still one of the most popular types of retirement savings plans.

Basically, annuities reverse regular life insurance policies: When you buy life insurance, you make regular payments to the company and your beneficiaries collect after your death. But with an annuity, you pay the cash now, or over a period of time, and collect on it later.

The single-premium deferred annuity is probably the most well known annuity product, especially for small investors. With these instruments, investors buy now and watch tax-deferred interest accrue. At some date in the future, you collect either a lump sum or receive regular payouts. These are the products that both Charter and Baldwin-United sold with great success until their parent companies ran into trouble.

Single-premium deferred annuities appeal to people with significant amounts of assets to tie up, and, generally, to people fifty and over.

Annuities don't come cheap. Some companies permit minimum investments of $5,000 on single-premium annuities, but others charge more; the average is $10,000. Another surprise to investors is the extensive charges: Typically, sales commissions range from 5 to 9 percent of the first year's premium, and your company will probably deduct an annual administrative fee, too. You can usually withdraw up to 10 percent annually of either your principal (what you initially invested) or the value at the beginning of the contract year (principal plus earnings). But above that, some companies may impose a charge of as much as 10 percent of the amount withdrawn.

Since annuities tie up a big chunk of cash for a long period, and because penalties can be steep, you, as an investor, want to be especially sure to do business with a reputable company.

"I suggest as a minimum that buyers look at the insurance company ratings of the A. M. Best Company," says Joseph M. Belth, professor of insurance at Indiana University. The company publishes *Best's Insurance Reports: Life/Health,* an independent rating guide. Public libraries should have the latest edition. However, the data on which the rankings are based are already months out of date at the time of publication.

"Under no circumstances," Belth continues, "should a person deal with a company not currently rated A-plus. If a person wants to be more conservative, then I suggest buying an annuity from a company only if it has ten consecutive years of top ratings by *Best's,*" Belth says.

"I wouldn't deal with a company whose ratings had slid or were dropped by *Best's,*" agrees J. Robert Hunter, director of the National Insurance Consumer Organization, a consumer activist organization based in Alexandria, Virginia. "I'd avoid buying an annuity from a new and innovative company. Ordinarily I like those sorts of companies, but not for a risky investment like an annuity." However, he notes, "If an old-line company like Prudential comes out with a new product, it's not the same as if it were from an untested company."

And he offers this advice: "Find out if the company is licensed in the state of New York, because New York has fairly stringent regulations. If it's licensed there, you can be pretty sure the company is watched carefully." *Best's* lists where the various companies are registered.

Learning about ratings and various products can consume a lot of your time. Independent insurance agents and brokerage firm salespeople will be able to tell you about a variety of annuities, and you'll do well to consult more than one.

Although it appears today that most companies that sell annuities are financially sound, if you ever learn that your company faces serious financial woes, deciding what to do will be as difficult as deciding which product to buy in the first place.

"The state insurance department won't be much help," Belth says. "All they will tell you is whether the company is licensed or not to do business in your state."

Information can prove extremely difficult to obtain and your two alternatives—pulling your money out and paying the penalties, or leaving it alone and praying for a happy ending—may seem equally unpleasant. However, accepting penalties may be preferable to having your money tied up at low rates.

As a final warning, Hunter advises that investors diversify: "Don't depend on just one annuity for your future."

PART FOUR

So You Want to Be a Millionaire?

JUST about anyone would feel more financially secure with $1 million in the bank.

You might think that a brilliant investment strategy, blind luck, or a rich uncle is what it takes to ring up this kind of net worth, but you would be mistaken.

Millionaire watcher and Georgia State University marketing professor, Thomas Stanley, has been tracking the nation's affluent for the last thirteen years. His eye-opening observations on what makes a millionaire follow in this interview:

Q: If I decided right now that I wanted a million dollars—and not a penny less—what's the first thing I should do?

A: Work, and work *more*. Becoming a millionaire is a very slow, very patient process. Most don't become millionaires before they reach their fifties. The person typically owns his own business or has substantial equity in the business he works for. A lot of them have become millionaires because they own the buildings their businesses are in. Commercial property appreciates in value without the IRS taking the lion's share.

Q: What fields offer the best chance of becoming a millionaire?

A: Any field. Because it's generally not the paycheck that makes you rich; it's what you do with your time. Ambitious people schedule themselves so they can moonlight on the side. Some professionals, such as lawyers and physicians, earn extra income by lecturing, consulting, and serving as expert witnesses.

Q: What are today's hot areas of moonlighting?

A: It depends on what you have to leverage. Maybe you can take something you did in childhood—like collecting stamps—and turn it into a business. Or let's say you travel frequently to certain cities. Your contacts and knowledge of the local economies might put you in a good position to market products there.

Q: Did most millionaires have a seven-figure bank account in mind when they started?

A: Not at all. Most of them have been dwelling on their families and their work—not on money. Money to them is really just a report card on their achievments. You may talk to them for five hours and the subject doesn't even come up. Often millionaires tend to underestimate their wealth. Until they sit down and count it, they have no idea how much they have.

Q: Are there certain personality traits millionaires seem to share?

A: Generally I've found them to be charming and very articulate. They have a good grasp of "people skills"—things like speaking clearly, having a firm handshake, looking people in the eye. And they have an energy that reflects their enthusiasm for what they do. Also, they're disciplined in their use of time and in their health. It's rare that you'll find a millionaire who's overweight. I see lots of affluent people who have been in the military, especially the Marine Corps, which may be the most regimented.

Q: Is there reason to believe that millionaires are smarter than other people?

A: Typically they're people who have good—not outstanding—intellects and are well-rounded. I don't think they are geniuses by any stretch of the imagination. They're analytical and bright without being particularly intellectual. That's why they relate so well to other people.

Q: You found that four out of five millionaires are self-made. Why is that?

A: Those who succeed seem to have certain achievement and competitive needs. Often they've worked hard so their children wouldn't face a life as tough as they did. But their intention to give their children opportunities usually translates into making things easy for them. As a result, the second generation lacks incentive. The fact that Dad is providing actually lessens your chances of becoming a millionaire yourself. People tend to dissipate wealth that is handed to them. Sometimes there's an element of rebellion involved, as well. If the children see a parent devoting a great deal of time to accumulating wealth, they might get turned off to the whole concept of money.

Q: Is there a giveaway that a person is a millionaire?

A: I can never tell, and I've been studying them for years. It's impossible to know from their personal appearance. These are not flashy people. They're more likely to have a standard

American-made sedan than a high-priced imported sportscar. A high number live in middle-class neighborhoods or rural areas. They usually stay in the same place for a long time because that's where their contacts are.

Q: What luxury items do they buy?

A: One in ten owns a yacht. But for the most part, while millionaires are more able than other Americans to buy luxury products, they tend not to. People think of millionaires as something out of *Dallas* or *Dynasty*. In reality, the notion of conspicuous consumption is garbage. These people have enough self-confidence that they don't need to prop themselves up on the symbols of success. If you look at what they spend as a percentage of their worth, it's a lot less than for most people.

Q: Are there reasons for that beyond their humility?

A: Sure. The way they see it, they *can't* splurge. The millionaire's objective is to minimize realized income, which is highly taxed. So even though he or she may be accumulating wealth, in the form of unrealized income, he or she's not generating much spendable income. Millionaires typically are cash-poor. I remember one telling me he was sometimes so broke that he had to borrow money from his workers to buy lunch. The idea that millionaires have rolls of hundred-dollar bills in their pockets is just absurd.

Q: Are millionaires as good at investing their money as they are at making it?

A: Most invest conservatively, in things like real estate, pension plans, and profit sharing. At the highest levels of wealth, however, many borrow heavily for investment purposes. Aside from the money they make on investing, this forces them to save. The philosophy is that by tying up their money, they won't have to spend on things they don't need.

Q: You describe millionaires as being very self-reliant. Do they seek help, though, in handling their finances?

A: Half of them don't use anyone other than an accountant. But those with the most wealth often employ several advisors. There seems to be a positive correlation between a person's worth and the number of information sources he or she taps. This also includes how many periodicals they read.

Q: Once financially set for life, do millionaires just call it quits?

A: Not these folks. They're not the type to rest on their laurels. They might build other businesses, increase the size of their holdings, or set up charities. Most don't believe in early retirement. They don't see work as just a way to make money. To them it's a labor of love.

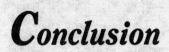

Conclusion

TAKING control of your finances is one of the most important facets of your life. Financial planning is simply a comprehensive, organized approach to this vital activity. Good intentions are not enough. You need a financial plan to keep pace with the changes that occur naturally in life.

A good financial plan is flexible. It provides for current needs, regardless of when you start your plan. But it's also adjustable to change. This enables you to build the secure financial future that should be your goal.

*I*ndex

INDEX

INDEX

INDEX